THE BREATH OF ODIN AWAKENS

By Frank A. Rúnaldrar

HIGH GALDR SERIES
Book One: The Breath of Oðin Awakens (2nd Ed)
Book Two: The Spirit of Húnir Awakens (Part 1)
Book Three: The Spirit of Húnir Awakens (Part 2)

QUESTIONS & ANSWERS SERIES
The Breath of Oðin Awakens - Questions & Answers

THE BREATH OF OÐIN AWAKENS

SECRETS OF THE NORSE HAMINGJA
&
LUCK-FUELLED BREATH
(2ND EDITION)

by
Frank A. Rúnaldrar

Part of the High Galdr Series
www.highgaldr.com

Published in 2017 by:
Bastian & West
www.bastianandwest.com

Part of High Galdr Series
www.highgaldr.com

ISBN: 978-0-9955343-4-6
(previous edition: 978-0-9955343-0-8)

A CIP catalogue record for this book is available from the British Library.

Cover design by: Judge a Cover Designs
In-book illustrations by: Ben Hansen

Book typeset in Niva Light by PeGGO Fonts, Norse font by Joël Carrouché and runic elements in Felt-Tip Futhark by Thomas Kaeding

I would like to dedicate this book to my family...

TABLE OF CONTENT

Secrets of the Norse Hamingja & Luck-Fulled Breath

Definitions of Norse Terms I
The Norse Tradition - Heritage of The Indo-Europeans..VII
   The Eddas.............................VII
   The Saga(s).............................x
Introducing... High Galdr..........................XIII
   What is Galdr?.............................XIII
The Norse Hamingja & Luck Fuelled Breath XVII

The Hamingja

Foundations of the Breath of Oðin - Hamingja & Megin..1
   What exactly is it?.............................2
The Hamingja at the Archetypal Level of the Self...9
The Mystery of Megin...............................13
   Mana of the Austronesians.............................14
   Manitou, Orenda and Other Terms used by the Native Americans...18

The Önd

Mastering the Hamingja.............................23
   Icelandic Rune Names.............................26
   High Galdr vs Simple Rune Chanting 27
Awakening the Hamingja.............................29
Hamingja for Protection 37
Personification of the Hamingja 41
Awakening the Core of the Self.....................55
Consciously Controlling the Personified Hamingja...63
Awakening the Breath of Oðin 71
Empowered Runic Vocalisation 83
   Megin-empowered Rune Chanting 84
   Dual-form Runic Vocalisation 87

APPENDIXES

APPENDIX A: TABLE OF RUNIC NAMES
   IN ICELANDIC & GERMANIC 95
APPENDIX B: REFERENCES & FOOTNOTES
   SUGGESTED FURTHER READING 99

OTHER TITLE BY FRANK A. RÚNALDRAR 105

FORTHCOMING TITLES 113

TABLE OF ILLUSTRATIONS

ARCHETYPAL LEVEL OF THE SELF 10
HAMINGJA LOCATION ON UPPER-BACK................31
ENHANCED PROTECTIVE FIELD...............................39
DNA CHARGED MEGIN FLOWING THROUGH
BLOODSTREAM 46
PERSONIFIED HAMINGJA FORMED BEHIND
THE PHYSICAL BODY (LIK)..58
PERSONALISED HAMINGJA SOLIDIFYING BY
SENSORY TRANSFER 66
DNA CHARGED & EMPOWERED MEGIN FLOW
HAMINGJA TO BODY AND VICE VERSA........................73
MEGIN USED TO EMPOWER RUNIC VOCALISATION 84

Notes From Publisher

It is with great pleasure that we are releasing the second edition of 'The Breath of Oðin Awakens'. Since taking over this title we have decided to rework certain internal and external parts which needed updating.

Essentially, no major changes to actual content have been made, other than a few corrections. Certain terminology changes were implemented to bring them in line with subsequent titles as well as a number of typographical updates. Illustrations have all been updated to bring their quality in line with those of other titles and a number of structural changes were made.

We hope you enjoy the freshly polished edition and continue to gain the benefits and insights so many readers have experienced.

DEFINITIONS OF NORSE TERMS

All terms used refer to their original Old Norse or Proto-Germanic meanings not their modern day derivatives in the Scandinavian, German or Icelandic languages.

Önd – Part of the psycho-spiritual construct of the Self as viewed in Norse mysticism and mythology, the Önd sits at the apex of the spiritual level of the Self and can be loosely described as 'The Breath of Oðin' or luck / Megin-fulled breath.

Óðr (or Óðr, or Óð) – Part of the psycho-spiritual Self-sitting at the apex of the mental part of the Self, it can be loosely thought of as the conscious awareness or totality of the spirit.

Hugr – The Hugr is often thought of as the reasoning or logic part of the mind, sometimes as the mind itself and often as the intellect or intellectual capacity of the mind. Essentially it is the manifestation of the active characteristics of the (Spirit) Óðr.

Minni – The polar opposite of the Hugr and often thought of as the root of memory, the Minni is actually the individual record of one's experiences and acts as an anchor point for those events.

Hamr – The Hamr is the energy body, often described as the blueprint of the physical.

Lik – Part of the psycho-spiritual Self sitting at the apex of the energetic part of the Self, the Lik is the complete physical body as a result of the fusion of matter and spirit via the medium of energy. When talking about the Lik we include everything which is part of it, including the energetic and spiritual elements as well as the typically physical ones such as blood, DNA, nervous system and so forth.

Sal – Part of the psycho-spiritual self sitting at the bottom of the energetic part of the Self, the Sal is often loosely translated as the 'shadow'. In effect, it is the complimentary opposite of the Hamr.

Heimdall – One of the principle Gods in Norse mythology, Heimdall was described as the white god or whitest of the gods. He is linked to light and the pure power thereof. He possesses the resounding horn Gjallarhorn, which he will sound at the time of Ragnarök. He is the God responsible for originating the various classes of mankind and imbuing these with increasing degrees of divinity.

The Æsir – This refers to the clan of Gods from Ásgarð, typically associated with the divine aspects of spiritual origin. They are wielders of the Galdr sciences (use of runes and their correct applications) and have strong connections with the spiritual, awareness, intellect, mind, knowledge and the sciences.

The Vanir – The Vanir refers to the clan of Gods from Vanaheim, typically associated with the natural order of things and having strong connections with nature, the world and the physical as it moves towards the spiritual. They are wielders of Seidr crafts (sorcery, divination, soothsaying, shamanistic practices, herbal medicines and so forth).

Yggdrasil (Mjötvið) – The mythical Ash tree that is home to the nine worlds in Norse cosmology. It is also thought of as being the foundation of the cosmos itself and everything within it.

Egil's Saga – Otherwise termed in Iceland as the Egla, this is an Icelandic Saga dating back to 1240 AD, which details the life of Egil Skallagrimsson a farmer, Viking and poet.

Muspelheim – Muspelheim was the first world to be formed out of the great emptiness called Ginnungagap. It is a realm of flame, fires, light and explosive power unreachable by any not native to it.

Húnir (Hœnir) – One of the Æsir Gods, he helped create mankind along with Oðin and Lóðurr. He gave the first man and woman Óðr and hence imbued them with spirit. He is also one of the Gods who survives Ragnarök and gains prophetic powers thereafter.

Njörðr – Vanir god of the Sea, he is the father of Freya and Frey and was one of the hostages exchanged in the Æsir-Vanir war. It is said he will return to head the Vanir after Ragnarök.

Lóðurr (Lóð or Lóðr) – Lóðurr is a mysterious God, whom academics seem unable to accept other than trying (and failing) to identify him with Loki or even Freyr. He gives the first man and woman blood and hence health, in other words flesh or physicality.

Ragnarök – Also known as the Twilight of the Gods, this final battle was foretold in the Völuspá (stanza 41). It describes the ultimate fate of the Gods themselves.

Ætts – Meaning 'clan', it can also refer to related grouping of concepts, individuals or sets of people. It is sometimes referred to as kin-Ætts which would be used in terms of a grouping of related people. For instance, Ætts in terms of individuals would include related individually such as family, whereas kin-Ætts would expand this to a wider set of relations such as an entire clan.

Norns – This typically refers to the Jotun (giantess) sisters Urð, Verðandi and Skuld who weave the threads of fate for men and gods alike. They also draw water from the Well of Urð and collect sands from around it to pour on the Yggdrasil to prevent it from rotting. The word Norn can also refer to the concept of the fate weaver attached to individuals at birth which could be either good or bad, weaving either a fortunate or unfortunate fate for that individual.

Niflheim – One of the Nine Worlds in Norse Cosmology, Niflheim is a world of primordial ice and cold, sometimes also called the mist world.

Fylgja – Part of the archetypal level of the Self, the Fylgja is a spirit which binds to the individual, becoming a part of him or her upon birth. It is always inherited down the ancestral lines and carries experiential essence and memories and powers of the former Self's embodiment. The Fylgja forms into either animal, humanoid or geometric form depending on evolutionary progress of both the individual and itself.

Kin-Fylgja – Similar to the Fylgja, this overarching spirit carries the experiential essences of the entire family line, the sum resulting from the entire ancestral lines up to the current point. It attaches to the eldest male of the family line and communicates primarily through the females of the line.

Hamingja – The Hamingja is part of the archetypal level of the Self. It manifests as an energetic organ in the individual which stores the Megin (power) it produces from various runic and life energies.

Wyrd and Ørlǫg – This refers to fate or rather threads of fate as they flow through creation. Cosmically, Ørlǫg is seen as infinite fibres of energetic substance flowing throughout all existence. From a human perspective, these fibres appear to flow through Creation but also through individuals, Gods and all life forms, setting the path they will follow over the course of their existence. However, when viewed from a Cosmic perspective, all things in Creation flow through the fibres. The Wyrd refers to these threads on a larger scale such as for humanity as a whole, individual races and clans while Ørlǫg refers to how these threads manifest on the individual level. The Wyrd is formed by the Norns and the Ørlǫg is build from the Wyrd based on individual's power, fate and evolutionary needs by the Fylgja.

Óðrerir (Odhrærir, Óðrørir) – This refers to the container or cauldron which holds the sacred mead. Its equivalent is the legend of the 'Holy Grail' in Arthurian mythology and the 'Holy Chalice' in Christian mythology. The Óðrerir may well have been the inspiration for these later myths.

THE NORSE TRADITION - HERITAGE
OF THE INDO-EUROPEANS

It is impossibly difficult to determine the full extent of or to search out all sources of the Norse tradition. Most pre-date the widespread availability of writing, while others were passed exclusively from one generation to the next orally. The main sources of knowledge left to us in this modern day and age are found in the Eddas and the Sagas.

THE EDDAS

The term 'Eddas' comes from Old Norse and it is used by modern-day students and academics to refer to two main Icelandic literary works that serve as the basis of our knowledge of Norse mythology, tradition, teachings and history.

There are two primary Eddas, both written during the 13th Century in Iceland. The first set is grouped under the label 'Poetic Eddas', which predate even the Viking Age, and come from an unknown source.

They are divided into two sections; the first is a narration of the creation, destruction and rebirth of the world and provides the mythology of the Norse deities as well. The second is a set of legends relating to Norse heroes, kings and wise men.

The Poetic Eddas were incorporated into the Codex Regius written during the 13th century. Unfortunately, it was not until the mid-1600s that the Codex resurfaced in the hands of Brynjólfur Sveinsson, a bishop to the Church of Iceland in Skálholt. Brynjólfur was also a scholar at heart, hence his fascination with the old myths and legends! It is he who collected and produced this compilation of Old Norse mythology and heroic poems into the Eddas. However, it is widely accepted that he was not their author and so they were not labelled after him. He gifted his findings to King Christian IV of Denmark in manu-script form, thus earning it the name Codex Regus, which was then preserved in the Royal Library until 1971 when a formal return was made to Iceland.

The second Eddas were compiled from traditional oral sources and (theorised to be derived from) an unknown set of Eddas often referred to as the Elder Eddas by Icelandic scholar Snorri Sturluson (dated from the 14th century). He collated these literary works under the label of Prose Eddas. Like the Poetic Eddas, the Prose Eddas also describe in detail the creation, destruction and rebirth of the world, Norse mythology and life. Due to his background and the time period in which Snorri lived, the 'Christianisation' of certain concepts and legends are to be found in this text. Nonetheless, it does provide an invaluable and rich account of the Norse tradition and, just as importantly, how it was recounted over the generations.

Scholars have long held the view that the Poetic Eddas, and therefore the Prose Eddas, came from a much older source. The rediscovery of what is known as the Elder Eddas helped confirm that suspicion. The Elder Eddas are comprised of the Pagan poems and teachings that were later hinted at in Snorri's Prose Eddas.

Many translations from Old Norse can be found and the number thereof seems to increase steadily over time. One key point to keep in mind is that the Eddas are complex literary works detailing the Norse tradition through poetry and prose. Accordingly, when reading various translations, different terms and words are often found to express the same underlying concept or similar words are used to describe totally different ones. Add to this the fact that many Old Norse terms have no equivalents in modern day languages, and it becomes vitally important to read in between the lines, so to speak, referring back to the concept rather than relying strictly on the words themselves. A literal, legalistic reading that has become completely engrained in the modern readers' minds will fail to capture the actual meanings, concepts and knowledge held within the Eddas.

Aside from those mentioned, other so-called Eddas can be found. These are typically adaptations in use by specific groups based on either the Prose or Poetic Eddas. The key point to note, however, is that those are adaptations.

The translations of the Prose and Poetic Eddas that have been used as source materials for this work can be found in both the references and further reading sections. Modern day adaptations and/or derivatives are not used.

THE SAGA(S)

Unlike the Eddas, the term Saga (story) refers to one of the many stories, poems, legends and so forth. Not all the Sagas made it into the Eddas. Individual Sagas might have not been discovered until a much later, post-Eddas compilation period.

These Sagas are individual tales in prose or poetic form detailing historical events of heroic deeds, tales or important persons (a great many of them Vikings, Pagans or even sometimes Christians), bishops, saints and even legendary heroes. Many of the Sagas include tales of kings, special individuals (such as the Egil Sagas used in this text), and even territorial historic events ranging from the Nordic countries to the British Isles, France and even North America (Canada in particular)[1]. Their main characteristic is that they are a historical statement or tale (that is the literal meaning of the term Saga). This has raised much speculation as the intellectual machinery attempts to digest material that is these days considered to be supernatural or metaphysical.

This range of subject matter is simply due to the fact that these records were, more often than not, kept within individual families, transmitted orally or simply brought from a different territory. Remember, the Old Norse people (Indo-Europeans) existed long before the Viking age and had to survive forced Christianisation, dispersion of territories, hostile natural environments, and so forth. In other words, these Sagas provided additional insights into the traditions, mythology, legends and teachings that were initially transmitted orally and then, once writing became widely available, were from time to time published. Even to this date, however, many of the Sagas have never been published and are kept from public view for a variety of reasons. Some of these reasons are of a very practical nature. In Iceland, for instance, these stories are considered to be part of the national heritage, hence books or manuscripts that are valued as family heirlooms, if known about, would be confiscated by the state on the basis of it being a national treasure. This is somewhat of an over-simplification but is an example of one of the many reasons why a lot of these Sagas never have (and most probably never will) see the light of public accessibility or dissemination. Others might hold deep-seated hereditary knowledge, which, more often than not, requires specific genetic and energetically transmitted capabilities to be of any use. This is the case with the higher mysteries bestowed upon the Jarls by Heimdall.

Fortunately, many Sagas are available for public consumption, and they do provide an exceptional insight into the wisdom and traditions of our ancestors. In this work, the Sagas are used to illustrate and gain further insights into teachings from older sources, be they part of the oral tradition or those in the Eddas[2].

This seeming endless diversity of sources is what makes studying the Old Norse tradition wildly exciting and fascinating beyond expectation, yet also insanely frustrating. Each Saga and Edda can expand our understanding, yet finding the relevant ones can be a most noteworthy challenge, in addition to actually understanding the knowledge therein once it is found! Nevertheless, gaining a solid foundation into the tradition is key; it is after all part of our heritage and is what empowers us. The appendices will provide more references and recommended reading. Fear not, however — all Eddas and Sagas relevant to the topics and teachings in this book have been included; for without basing such teachings in the actual texts and other sources of heritage they would hold no validity per se. It is of vital importance to work with these Eddas and Sagas as the foundation upon which we build our spiritual heritage.

Introducing... High Galdr

The Breath of Oðin is one of the key skills required for mastery of High Galdr. The knowledge and teachings provided in here serve to awaken one of the most important parts of the Self: the Hamingja. The mastery of the Self, as defined by our Norse ancestry, unlocks the potential for Galdr. This involves the awakening of the Önd, developing the flow of conscious awareness of the Óðr and embodying the Self in the Sal and Hamr. In these pages, the Mysteries of the Önd (the Breath of Oðin) are described plainly and clearly without symbolic linguistics or mystic cloaking.

What is Galdr?

The practice of Galdr is fundamental to the Æsir and was 'taught' to humankind when Heimdall revealed the runes to mankind. Subsequently, other teachers from the realms of Ásgarð came forth to various gifted individuals to teach them more advanced applications of runic practices. Long ago, Galdr was taught to the Vanir by Oðin himself, just as they revealed the arts of Seidr to him. Interestingly this exchange is an excellent illustration of the practical applications of X Gjöf (Gebo) (the principle of a gift requiring a gift) even at that divine level!

So what is Galdr? One can define it as the uttering of runes, runic formulae, runic chants, the vocalisation of runes and bind-runes accompanied by their tracing or carving.

In Midgard, and specifically in relation to humans, these arts were used in a severely limited fashion, which essentially reduced Galdr to vocalisation of the runes. It became a meagre chanting, visualising and tracing of the runes (for the sake of brevity, formulae, chants and bind-runes are herein included when mentioning 'runes'). Worse yet, the concept of Galdr itself has been fused with that of Seidr. This merging was not done through a harmonious blending of the two arts, but rather aspects of the one were muddled into the other. The underlying fundamentals of Galdr gradually shifted from pure mysticism to one of ritualistic application, in the process losing the true power of Galdr itself, which wound up as a shadow of its former potential.

Some might argue that elements of Seidr are needed in Galdr, such as the induction of trance states found within Seidr as being essential to the effective use of Galdr. This is both partly correct and incorrect. The correct part is that trance mastery is essential to Galdr, but it is also incorrect to assume that Seidr is required. Galdr itself is used to induce a trance state, which can at times even surpass those achieved via Seidr (in terms of practicality not potential). This stems from the mystical aspects of Galdr, and is the reason why it was deemed in the days long past to be the sacred science of the Gods.

The 'High Galdr' series seeks to bring back the knowledge and the tools to practice the sacred aspects of Galdr. Due to its nature, some will flock to it, others will seek to master it and yet more will seek to abuse it. To the former, all that remains to be said is, be persistent and practice; even partial success and minor achievements expand the Self, providing phenomenal gains. Once fully mastered, there will be nothing left anyone in Midgard can teach. For the latter, a warning: even though 'High Galdr' can be misused, it is vital to remain aware that the Gods protect their mysteries and they themselves throw hurdles in the path and practices of those who are seeking to harm their people, their creation and the cosmic order of things for which they are responsible. Not much else needs to be mentioned on the subject other than to confirm that no matter how hard those who would abuse them try, these sacred mysteries will always evade mastery.

In these pages, will provide instructions to take the first steps. It will assist in uncovering the mysteries of this science and awaken the parts of the Self (and moving them towards the divine) to eventually uttering the Galdr across multiple levels of reality (both sub-jectively and objectively). This will free the mind of all the baggage that inhibits our heritage from blooming, enabling you to learn the rune and each rune's specific energy patterns, condense them into reality, and finally unleash them. The microcosmic Yggdrasil within our bodies and the macrocosmic Yggdrasil will be brought into a synchronous harmony as the Self unfolds into its divine birth right.

Now is the time to take that first breath;
Now, the 'Breath of Oðin' awakens.
May the Önd be strong within!

Frank A. Rúnaldrar

The Norse Hamingja & Luck
Fuelled Breath

In this, the first work dealing with the Norse views of the Self, we are going to look at two concepts which can be termed the archetypal level of the Self, composed of the Önd, Hamingja and Fylgja. We will specifically focus on the first two: the Önd and the Hamingja. The Fylgja is a vast subject in its own right and will be dealt with separately.

When looking at the Self, one has to deal with two fundamental concepts: characteristics and power. Out of the nine parts of the psycho-spiritual Self, three of them deal with intangible inanimate characteristics or properties and the remaining six pertain to animate powers or forces (substances). The unification of these nine parts with our core or 'Spark of Self' produces the 'Divine Self'. The triple triangular division of the Norse Self illustrates core parts of the Self (namely, the Önd, Óðr and Lik) quite well, as they are either inflowing or outflowing powers of the characteristics thereof. This will be dealt with in detail later on. In terms of the current focus, the Önd is the apex point of the archetypal manifestation of the Self, as both an inflowing and outflowing principle. If this seems confusing, this concept will become clear once the practical work is undertaken. For this reason, discussions of this aspect of the Self will be set aside until the second part of this work. For now, the historical aspect will suffice to ground understanding.

The breath (Önd) (which means megin-fuelled breath) is one of Ođin's gifts to the first man (Ash) and woman (Embla). It has been passed down through generations ever since. What this mysterious breath is has never been fully understood. Despite this, it is a fundamental quality of the Self. Unlike normal breathing, it is not connected with the physiology of the human being (well, not directly). Its significance cannot be grasped by mere intellectualisation of the word Önd or searching for 'correct' translations and so forth. Its deeper meaning eludes the grasp of the intellect, leaving only a metaphorical concept. In order to approach the meaning of this mystery, one has to struggle with the following concept: that the core of the Self, the spark that is at the root of our very individuality, is alive without the need for a spirit, a body or anything else between; it is a pure crystal-lisation of Being (this belongs to the mysteries of ⚡Sól (Sowilo)).

Once it has been awoken, what the Breath of Ođin does is to allow for a breath to flow in and out of the core of our Being. The Hamingja and the energy it produces (Megin) are crucial to unleashing this breath; it is the actual characteristics of the totality of Önd. The stronger the Hamingja, the more powerful the Megin and the stronger the flow of Önd, which will eventually change from a fluid expression of the qualities of the core to an actual force expressing its very nature throughout creation. This in turn will unify all the parts of the Self into a cohesive whole and awaken the 'Spark of Self' to full awareness. For those with a metaphysical background, it can be understood as the Breath of Oðin allowing the core of the Self to 'breathe out' through the planes, initially into the spiritual, then into the energetic and finally into the physical, all facilitated through the Hamingja via the pathways of each individual's DNA.

THE HAMINGJA

FOUNDATIONS OF THE BREATH OF ODIN - HAMINGJA & MEGIN

The Hamingja, as defined by traditional teachings, is one of the most mysterious and yet underestimated parts of our psycho-spiritual constructs. It is of the highest importance, as it makes us unique in terms of life forms. The Hamingja is the key to our ability to generate Megin, that often elusive yet fundamental energetic essence which allows for miracles, evolution and life to take place, and for the cosmic mysteries to unfold without restraint.

Making comparisons between different traditions can be troublesome and allows for the bleeding of foreign elements into the original. More often than not, the intellectual analysis of similar concepts and ideologies results in a dangerous assumption of equivalence between the subjects being compared. Such assumptions should be avoided at all costs. However, this is one of the times when an exception to the non-comparative rule should be made, partly for two reasons. The first is that when looking at the Hamingja, it is unique to the Norse tradition yet most humans have one. It is a fundamental criterion of taking on human form and life. Due to this uniqueness, the concept and its use are very misunderstood and rather difficult to grasp. The other reason is the need to understand fully what the Hamingja is, its importance and its use. To do so, one needs to understand what it produces: Megin (as known to those of Norse heritage). Our ancestors understood this force as being mysterious and almost mystical in nature, and has been typically called 'Norse Luck', charisma and so forth. Since this force is universal and present in all human beings, it is advantageous to look at how other traditions that developed, without the interference of Christianisation, understood it.

WHAT EXACTLY IS IT?

In practice, understanding the nature and purpose of the Hamingja is the first step in gaining a solid grasp of it. Typically, these mysteries are first grasped intellectually. The intellect has a limit, however, and practical experience is key to mastery. The Hamingja is described as:

> "According to Northern lore, Megin is stored in an energy construct within the aura of a human being called the Hamingja. Numerous references are made to the Hamingja of Northern heroes and kings in the sagas, . . ."[3]

The concepts of both the Hamingja and the Megin it produces are introduced in this quote. So, let us examine these two in greater depth...

Interestingly, and as pertains to our discussion, Andy Orchard (an academic in old English, Norse and Celtic literature) notes that the Hamingja can take a female form, as did Rudolf Simek, an Austrian Germanist and philologist who translated into German five of the Norse Sagas and specialised in the history of Germanic people, the Viking Age and Germanic mythology. In the Sagas of Egil[4], the Hamingja is also described as being able to appear in female form.

The Víga-Glums saga mentions this again when Glúmr, after the death of his maternal grandfather, dreamed of a gigantic woman coming to visit and join him. This was interpreted as the Hamingja, post-death of its owner, being given to Glúmr. You might be wondering whether it is possible to have multiple Hamingja; the answer is a simple yes. G. Dumézil[5] points out that it is typically a sign of great power to have several Hamingja. The sword transfer described in the Víga-Glums sagas is where Vígfuss receiving a second Hamingja as a sword is a typical symbolic representation of this kind of transference.

Unlike with the Fylgja, the Hamingja can also be bestowed onto another while the possessor is still alive. This is shown in the Göngu-Hrólf Saga where King Hreggviðor turns all the luck and courage that followed him over to his son-in-law by an act of will (more on this in the discussions of initiations). Why would this be possible? Simply because the Hamingja specifically is not animistic but the form taken is far more symbolic of the type of Megin (force/power/energy) that it embodies.

These hints at the personification of the Hamingja are central to these teachings and of importance to the practical work herein. Their importance is touched upon in the Rune Mentalist Skills which states:

"We can say that the amount of Luck in your life is the equivalent to the amount of Megin concentrated in your Hamingja or psychic energy reservoir.

It is common that people experience the best of their Luck in the early years of life. That is when the Hamingja is fresh and full of Megin that is rightfully yours [...] through your share of the energy 'treasury' of your family ancestral stream. Because of this, things happen naturally and effortlessly and you experience any number of 'lucky' synchronicities early in life."[6]

The Hamingja, unlike the Fylgja, is not a natural host of consciousness; rather, it is necessary to work on imbuing it with awareness and taking control of it. That is what awakens its full potential and our awareness of it. Awakening the Hamingja will hyperactivate it and its production of Megin. This in turn empowers all that you do and starts to activate the mysterious Önd (known in Ásgarð as the Breath of Oðin).

Very few types of beings have a Hamingja. Mankind is one of the rare exceptions and so are the Gods. Other beings such as archons, egregores and thought forms (even those that are thought of as being divine) lack this psycho-spiritual construct and are therefore unable to produce Megin. At death, since it detaches when various components of the Self separate, humans lose their Hamingja with certain notable exceptions. The uniqueness of humans and their Hamingja are the envy of creation itself. That is the main reason why so many beings, including a large number of spirits, created beings and even those referred to as 'aliens' prey upon the human Self. It is also one of the reasons so few life forms are creative. Megin is needed to create, infuse and empower. A very interesting exceptionality is found in human Hamingja since humans are formed out of Midgard, which is the central point in Yggdrasil; this enables the human Hamingja to inherit those qualities of centrality and the ability to process any of the energies of the Nine Worlds rather than being limited to just one.

It is best to think of the Fylgja-Hamingja mechanism as a maturation of potential in terms of countless millennia of evolution, with each generation growing in ability, knowledge, experience and power accumulated in the ancestral lines. Each child is born with a fragment of this totality of potential in order to evolve it further and upon death, the Fylgja collects his or her memory and experiential knowledge which produce the life force of the ancestry. The Hamingja, a manifestation of that individual's accumulated energetic dynamism, can be passed on by the will of the individual or naming. There has never been reincarnation per se, and the Norse tradition recognises that fact well. It is nothing more than a modern concept used to make the prospect of dying less devastating. Instead, the shift of the Fylgja-Hamingja up and down the generational lines allows for a continuation of the fruits of labour from one generation to the next, each life adding to the previous and manifesting in the future. Ultimately, this leads to individuals being born with the ability to manifest more and more of the total potential of their ancestral lines until an individual is born with the innate ability to manifest the original divine characteristics contained therein. Egil's Saga[7] illustrates this principle well, in which the Gods bestow the Hamingja upon their children and get directly involved in manipulating their lives. Additionally, in the Norse tradition, the first child of a God is not a wonderfully powerful individual but rather frail and weak; it is only through successive generations that more and more of the innate divinity gains expression.

A perfect example of this is found in the story of the siring of the three types of humans by the God Heimdall is found in the Rígsþula ('Lay of Rig'), one of the Eddic poems. This is one of the stories of Ríg (another name for Heimdall) and how he fathered mankind. Incidentally, this is also attested in the Völuspá, the first poem of the Poetic Eddas.

The account goes as follows: While walking along a shore, Ríg comes to the hut owned by Ái (great-grandfather) and Edda (great-grandmother). He is offered food and lodging, eventually spending the night in between the couple in bed and siring a child. This child was named Þræll, meaning thrall, serf or slave. Eventually, this child's offspring became the race of serfs. As Ríg travelled further, he came across a house where he met Afi (grandfather) and his wife Amma (grandmother). They offered him a good meal, after which he once more ended up sleeping in between the couple, siring another child. This second son was named Karl, meaning freeman, whose offspring in turn became the ancestors of free farmers, craftsmen and traders. Travelling on, Ríg reached a mansion where he met Faðir (Father) and Móðir (Mother). They offered him an opulent meal, following which he yet again found himself in their bed and slept in between them. He sired another son. This time, Móðir named the baby Jarl, meaning earl/noble, who was of fair hair and bright white in colour (bleikr). After he grew up, Ríg appeared to him and claimed him as his son and gave him his own name: Ríg (note the importance of naming in transferring Hamingja down the generations; more on this below). He not only made him his heir but also taught him the secrets of the runes after bestowing his name upon him (hence his Hamingja) and guided him to seek out lordship. And thus were seeded the three types of humans imbued with various degrees of divinity.

In this tale, we see how the Þræll (or Thrall) were limited, the Karls had fewer limits and finally the Jarls became kings and wise men who were capable of runic learning. It was impossible for the Gods to teach the runes and their mysteries to the Thralls and the Karls but they did so very efficiently with the Jarls due to this potentiation of divinity within which requires not only the DNA (genetics) but also the power (via Hamingja). This generational growth occurs as a result of transference and the accumulation of experiences. In turn, this force (the power via Hamingja) grows through each consecutive Self, embodying fractions of the totality of ancestral potential. This process can be observed in parents, who pass on the results of entire lifetimes of learning, experience, development and spiritual and mental growth to their offspring. For example, when compared to others, some people are born with seemingly incredible abilities; those are just the practical results of this hereditary evolution via ancestral lines. There are exceptions but those are so rare that there is no point in discussing them here.

All of this being said, from a practical point of view the primary concern is to take control of the Hamingja, awaken it, form it and develop its full function. Once anyone achieves a full awakening, the ability of other beings to tap into its Megin is immediately locked down. Instead, the Megin is funnelled into the Self's own evolution and the circulating of the Önd. This is one of the main reasons why mankind has been kept in the dark about its functions and abilities.

THE HAMINGJA AT THE ARCHETYPAL LEVEL OF THE SELF

It is impossible to look at the Hamingja in total isolation without losing the important relationships within the Self construct. As can be seen from the diagram below, the Hamingja shares a very close and important relationship with the Fylgja as well as the Önd. The relationship between the Fylgja and the Hamingja is often hinted at within the Eddas. Essentially it is simple: the Fylgja uses the Megin produced by the Hamingja to fuel itself and do its work. However, the relationship with the Önd is far more obscure and less well known in Midgard. It is typically dormant and unable to awaken or be active in those who are purely focused on the mundane; there simply is no modus operandi for such activity to take place. Once awakened, it starts to flow through the Hamingja and the Fylgja imbuing them with a personalised divine essence. This will be covered in more detail in the practical exercises.

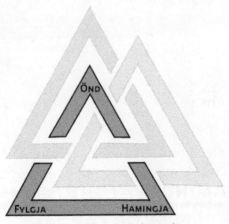

Archetypal level of the Self

There is an additional important relationship to be considered: that of the Hamingja <—> Hugr <—> Hamr. Those who have studied through the 'Norse Self' will note that this is another triangular relationship that links all parts of the Self governable by the conscious (or rather all manifestations of the functioning of the conscious). It is fascinating that these three should be the Hamingja, the mind or logic / reasoning capacity (Hugr) and the energetic blueprint of our physical body (Hamr). Compare this relationship with the 'subconscious' one of Fylgja <—> Minni <—> Sal. All these are 'subconsciously' controlled parts of the Self and vehicles for the manifestation of our consciousness across realities: the vessel for faring forth (Fylgja), the experiential manifestation of our lives (Minni) and the shadow body (Sal).

Due to the nature of the Hamingja <—> Hugr <—> Hamr relationship, enhancing the Hamingja will have a direct effect on the other two. It is important to keep in mind that, in practice, this relationship requires the Hamingja to be shaped in accordance to the shape of our physical bodies (Lik) (in accordance to the Hamr). Working with this aspect of the Self brings greater expansion of intellectual abilities.

The final matter to keep in mind on the topic of relationships within the Self is to note that the triangle of the archetypal level (as illustrated above) eventually becomes the foundation upon which the Divine Self is formed. Hence the Fylgja and Hamingja work is not only essential but forms the basis from which the rest of the Self rises and on which it depends. This is one of the key reasons why so much effort and so much information for these two parts of our psycho-spiritual constructs is provided in comparison with the others.

When working at the archetypal level of the Self, each and every part is an expression of 'Will' in some form or another. The Hamingja, as an expression of willpower, is a direct manifestation of the actual power aspect of the personal will, the drive to move forward, the force behind motivations and the 'will to fight' for what is aimed at or desired. Have you ever noticed how, for some people, those few things that they fight for tooth and nail in their youth become nothing more than a faded dream later on in life? That is a typical effect of the fading of Megin, which dulls the drive to achieve that goal due to a shortage of Megin energy.

On the other hand, the Fylgja, expresses the will of the ancestral line which works through the individual. Those who have a strong family bond will understand this all too well. They express it as part of their identity. This is typically exemplified by the use of 'Son of X' or 'Daughter of X'. The new generation is ultimately an embodiment of the family line up to this particular point in time and space, and the Fylgja expresses the will of this lineage working through the individual in order to manifest fully and grow further.

The Önd is even more significant. It is the expression of the pure abstract archetypal 'spark' of Self and the flow of the Önd is a direct manifestation of this pure undiluted will (for want of a better term). It is the will of one's essence, the absolute manifestation of individuality and the purpose for existence and all that this particular Self is. This is the will that is the root of our very manifestation when we stand at the central point of creation and say, 'I am', 'I am that which I am' and 'I do that which I do'. This is the expression of the will working through the Önd which is empowered and manifested by it. The pure 'I', at the highest level of being, speaks through the unfolding Önd currents.

For this reason, awakening of the megin-fuelled breath (Önd) is the ultimate awakening.

THE MYSTERY OF MEGIN

Prior to looking at the practical side of things, it is important to understand what it is you are seeking to achieve. A lot of information that is required has unfortunately been lost due to the suppression of the Norse tradition and spirituality. The following is stated in Rune Mentalist Skills:

> ". . . in Northern lore this universal energy is given a uniquely individualized identity. When specifically addressed as the energy within an individual, this energy is called Megin. Megin is defined as a personal force distinct from physical power or strength, the possession of which assures success and good fortune. It equates to what is called 'charisma', but much more than just everyday charm, popularity, or ability to persuade as defined in the dictionary."[8]

To understand Megin, a comparative study of age old traditions which predate mainstream religions is needed. It is interesting to ponder why it has not been explored in mainstream religions? Given that this energy has been around for so long, is fundamental to life, and must have been known for longer than 2,000 years. The best place to start looking is at traditional and linguistic systems also rooted in animism that ran parallel to those in existence during the proto-Norse period. Three parallel concepts to that of Megin can be found: 'mana' from the Austronesian languages (a language family, which has been extensively studied as a topic in cultural anthropology, spoken in Southeast Asia, Pacific islands and the Madagascar), the concept of 'orenda' (a mana equivalent) and the concept of 'manitou' from the Native Americans.

MANA OF THE AUSTRONESIANS

Mana is found in the Austronesian and proto-Austronesian linguistic system. In the cultures of the Pacific Islands, the term mana is associated with 'power, effectiveness and prestige' of a supernatural origin[9]. Post-exploration by Westerners, it has found a place in cultural anthropology, which explored links to western animism and subsequently pre-animism.

During the Polynesian Lexicon project[10], researchers found that the word mana existed in proto-Oceanic languages where the term originally meant "powerful forces of nature such as thunder and storm winds" that were conceived as the expression of an unseen supernatural agency. As Oceanic-speaking peoples spread eastward, the notion of an unseen supernatural agency became detached from the physical forces of nature that inspired it and assumed a life of its own[11]. The concept of mana being part of the fundamental underlying energetic makeup of natural phenomena makes a regular appearance.

In Melanesian culture (a people who derived from African emigrants between 50,000 and 100,000 years ago), specifically in anthropology and folklore studies, the first sustained description of mana is found, whereby it is defined as "a force altogether distinct from physical power, which acts in all kinds of ways for good and evil, and which it is of the greatest advantage to possess or control"[12]. For the Melanesians, mana extended further than just a type of mysterious/divine energy and went hand in hand with their concept of 'force' as coming from a spiritual being, 'the anima'.

In the work of Robert Randolph Marett[13], mana is proposed as being found in a pre-animistic form which is beyond culture and natural causes, be they physical or animistic, yet it flows through living beings. For example, athletes with the same mental and physical qualities would be distinguished by victory based on which of the two had more 'luck'. Here one finds a clear association between the concepts of mana and luck (as we have it in the Norse mysteries). There is a distinct symmetry between the Hamingja and the Megin which is referred to as mana. Megin (or mana) is infinitely competitive and aggressive to the extent where Megin from different sources will compete against each other as a matter of course (more on this later).

Marett delves further into the Melanesian views on mana, detailing how they considered it to be granted by animae, where animae was believed to be the 'souls' of men, ghosts of dead men and spirits appearing as and imitating men. The mana was believed to be given by a universal being but was also independent of it, which gave it some sort of energetic quality that could be produced by specific animae and then live on in objects, places and other people. He further specifies natural events as being imbued with mana. His list includes "startling manifestations of nature," "curious stones," animals, "human remains," "blood"[14] "thunderstorms, eclipses, eruptions, glaciers", and especially "the sound of the bullroarer"[15].

In Maett's view, mana is a distinct power obtained from the animae. This parallels very well with the qualities assigned to Megin. Much debate has subsequently been put in print regarding the universality (or lack thereof) of the concept of mana, with certain anthropologists arguing for and others against. This is of little concern since the concept of Megin is not only present in the Norse tradition but actually plays an important role both in terms of the life and evolution of our spirits, ancestral lines and so forth.

Before leaving the discussion of mana, it is worth looking at Polynesian cultures and their take on this concept. For them, it is said to be of supernatural origin, manifesting as a highly sacred and impersonal universal force. It is said to give power and authority, prestige and influence, and one can imbue essentially anything with it. Importantly, according to those cultures, it is gained at birth and through warfare. This partially parallels our concept of Megin, which is granted from the ancestral streams at birth. It is no coincidence that many ancient Vikings were of noble descent, mass conquerors and heavily invested in warfare. The topic of warfare and gaining mana from it will be not be covered in this text but will feature in subsequent materials.

We can also detect many pointers to the nature of mana within Hawaiian culture. It is seen not only as a type of spiritual energy but also as a healing power (which fits in well with Megin) that can be imbued in people, places and objects. Additionally, the Hawaiians held the view that all of our actions can either deplete or contribute to this store of available mana. They believed that in people, balanced action in synchronicity with the balance of nature will add to that store. This is an important concept when looking at being balanced, centred and in harmony.

In Hawaiian traditions, mana can be won through war and politics or through sex and peace. The gods Ku and Lono represent these two different pathways to accumulate each type of mana. These beliefs were reflected throughout their social traditions; even the ruler was subject to the two paths as he was believed to permeate the land with his mana, providing he followed the paths of righteousness and remained in balance with the Gods and the land itself. A ruler's passion for war provided one channel to accumulate mana (providing he was victorious and performed the correct rituals pre and post-war). The other means was that of sexual relationships and it was said that if a commoner was able to sleep with a ruler, he would gain that ruler's mana (note that a ruler's mana was considered superior to a commoner's).

In Norse tradition, any hint of the ruler's mana being depleted could cost him his throne. There is a good chance that loss of mana from the ruler allowed for the opportunity for a replacement to gain traction and power. Therefore, homosexual relationships with the ruler were discouraged, otherwise a man could take his mana / power and in effect dethrone him. This may explain why homosexual relationships have been made into a taboo by newer religions in this day and age. In terms of religious worship, a ruler had an obligation to transmit mana through acts of devotion to the Gods. If another man were able to gain the ruler's mana through sex he might not worship the same God(s) hence depriving the kingdom's deity of power (mana). This serves as a preventative measure to ensure that this superior type of mana is not passed onto someone who is not dedicated to the current religious establishments.

As a side note, it is interesting to look at the practices of the old families, where the High Chief would practice a Ni'aupi'o relationship, allowing for an offspring of brother-sister mating, which when producing an offspring would be considered to be a god incarnate. This was also a common practice amongst Egyptian royal families. It was seen as the way to protect and bolster the familial mana pool. Nowadays, such practices amongst siblings and close cousins are illegal in most countries around the globe.

MANITOU, ORENDA AND OTHER TERMS USED BY THE NATIVE AMERICANS

The concept of Megin also exists in the traditions of various Native American tribes and is known by the term 'orenda' or manitou. It refers to spiritual power, which is believed to be inherent in people and the environment they live in. Could this be a possible hint at the reason for humankind being part of the planet's life cycle? Anthropologist John Hewitt[16] describes activities in nature as being a "ceaseless struggle of one orenda against another, uttered and directed by the beings or bodies"[17] and as being the force behind miracles, divination, blessings, curses and other such supernatural phenomena[18]. This force was seen as lacking personification or collective power, however[19]. He also notes the same concept was being present in other tribes using a different term: the Sioux had 'wakd', while the Mohawk, Cayuga and Oneida tribes used the term 'karenna'. Other parallels are found in almost every Native American tribe. Interestingly, he also notes that this force can be used for good or ill. When used for 'malign, deadly, lethal or destructive purposes', it is referred to as otgon[20].

It is noteworthy that these tribes considered shamans as having a "great and powerful" orenda[21]. This quality determined winning or losing battles, similar to that of hunters and their prey. Maintaining balance is vital to the uninhibited flow of orenda in conjunction with orenda reserves so that the fullest and most effective use of it can be made.

Putting all of these various yet surprisingly similar concepts of mana, orenda and manitou together, we discover a supernaturally sourced type of force or energy — a source of power, prestige, authority, luck and healing that can be used for divine blessings and curses. This same power is also the causation of supernatural phenomena found behind the forces of nature and strong manifestations of natural events that are distinct from the strictly physical and can be used for good or ill by the 'beings' or bodies of living entities through which it flows. It can be embedded in people, objects and places and is independent of its source. It is believed to be gained at birth, during victories in war and through specific sexual practices, or through objects and places that have a strong quantity of it imbued within. Rulers and shamans are said to possess great quantities of this force, which in turn brings prosperity to those they rule or help.

Here you will find an expression of individual will that lends itself to success.

THE ÖND

MASTERING THE HAMINGJA

When working with the Hamingja, it is absolutely IMPERATIVE to stick with the outlined sequence. Rushing through one part to get to the more 'exciting' ones or skipping one due to difficulty is not an option. Why? Because this part of the Self is essentially responsible for fuelling all the other parts (even to a certain extent the physical, at this point) and is, technically speaking, an aspect of our 'subconscious' (connected with the ancestral collective or unconscious, as some would call it). The only way to gain any significant level of control is by gradually extending conscious influence over the Hamingja one step at a time, in order to prevent it feeling threatened or else it will very readily rebel and potentially cause harm. What we are dealing with here is an active aspect of the (divine level) 'subconscious' minds; that is, when trying to bring it within our conscious control, a bridging of the conscious and 'subconscious' aspects of the mind takes place. Additionally, the fact that those two parts of our own minds communicate using different systems (the one consists of thoughts, logic and reason, the other of instinct, feeling and memory). To make things even more complex, that part of our Self is used to being depleted by, let us call them, 'predators' and hence is not used to dealing with larger energy levels or the conscious directly (with some exceptions, such as with rune mystics and shamans). As the relationship between the two grows, these aspects of our mind start to merge and because the Hamingja produces Megin, changes can occur on any and all levels of our Self.

The following practices are set out to enable those who are patient and who persevere in their work to develop a fully-fledged Hamingja, which they will be able to fully interact with and eventually gain conscious influence over. It is important to keep in mind that development of the Hamingja is not in and of itself the ultimate goal, nor is the prevention of the loss of Megin. Rather, those should be considered as just initial steps towards the final end-product, which is awakening the Divine Self. Once the Hamingja is able to power other parts of our Self and the Fylgja has been fully integrated, the megin-fuelled breath (Önd) will start to awaken and stir into activity. This is the primary reason for its development. Be patient, consistent and thorough and never rush things.

The first step is to be balanced (having worked with your Fylgja will be of great assistance). If you have any inner issues, struggles or what are often termed heartaches, you should look into these before beginning Hamingja development. A strong mind and firm heart are needed for this work; strong emotional conflicts, deep emotional pain such as a hunger for vengeance, unresolved conflicts, unresolved loves and so forth will affect the Hamingja, its underlying behaviour and how it responds or fails to respond as the case may be. For instance, having anger issues or violent tendencies can result in a Hamingja, which, once developed, turns against you and is violent. Its fundamental manifestation will be one of violent behaviours and instinctive aggression, seeking out more fighting and causing violence. Everything else becomes secondary to such a 'personified' Hamingja. With a vast enough pool of Megin, a Hamingja can easily take over the rest of the Self and drive it to self-destruction. Hence, being in balance is the key. Dealing with underlying emotional issues is a must before this is undertaken. Good contact with the Fylgja and dealing with such issues is the key to gaining and re-maining in control.

There are some darker aspects to these practices, which we do not touch on here. Those practices are what one could describe as being in sync with the brutal, emotionless aspects of nature herself; they allow for a greater diversity of practice but also are open to all ranges of abuse. To wield those more intense aspects, a personified Hamingja requires full mastery of all the current methods.

There are phases in the following practices, which can be outlined as:

1 Awakening the Hamingja fully
2 Providing protection
3 Personifying the Hamingja
4 Awakening the core of the Self
5 Gaining and increasing control of the personified Hamingja

6 Awakening the Breath of Oðin

7 Expanding the production of Megin

8 Expanding consciousness with Megin

9 Empowering actions, thoughts and skills with Megin

Beyond these one would be delving into those advanced practices, which will be covered in a later publication; the current sections deal with items 1 to 7.

Icelandic Rune Names

The practical sections make use of the Icelandic rune names rather than the Germanic, primarily because Icelandic resonates more with what can be termed the 'cosmic' level modus operandi of the rune streams whereas the Germanic are more in tune with the Midgard level. When working with High Galdr, you should always use the Icelandic; when using simple runic invocations or bringing about some causal effect on the physical or earthly level of reality, then the Germanic is perfectly suitable.

It is for those who are not of Icelandic heritage somewhat more challenging to tap into those runic currents. However, not to worry; detailed instructions on how to amplify this 'connection' will be given at a later time. For the purposes of awakening the Breath of Oðin, either version can be used very effectively since the work is internal to the Self. Simply make use of whichever is more familiar. For this reason, the Germanic equivalents are always shown in parenthesis next to the Icelandic (Appendix A contains a reference table providing the equivalent names).

HIGH GALDR VS SIMPLE RUNE CHANTING

The upcoming practices were all developed and tested with both the unleashing of High Galdr runic power as well as by the use of simple rune chanting (with associated visualisations). It is important to keep in mind that they are intended to be used as a pre-requisite to learning High Galdr. Accordingly, the initial work with the Breath of Oðin is usually undertaken with simple runic chants. The High Galdr can be used for those who wish to repeat the practices using those mastered skill sets.

ᛋAWAKENING THE HAMINGJA

The strength or power of one's Hamingja is weakened due to its limited usage and lack of stress (or more correctly, friction). Using it as most do in a passive fashion and occasionally filling it with runic energy will not cause any degree of friction, which is needed to force it into action. Very much like a muscle in the physical body (Lik), if it is not exercised regularly or pushed, it will not grow and become subject to stasis and slumber.

The first step is to force growth. Fortunately, doing so is simplicity itself, as all parts of the Self want to and need to grow and evolve. Before delving into the exercises, you will need to establish contact with your Hamingja. Simply enter into a light meditative state, relaxing and allowing yourself to sink into a slight trance state. Having done so, feel the Hamingja as a type of container on your back; it sits in-between the shoulder blades and expands slightly downwards. Focus on it and will yourself to feel it. Will your perceptions of it to strengthen, focus awareness on it and send forth the desire to communicate. This is sufficient to raise a response. In case of trouble, using the ᛗ Maður (Mannaz), ᚠ Óss (Ansuz) and ᚠ Fé (Fehu) combination of runes in sequence will assist in refocusing the sensing.

ᛗᚠᚠ

The manner in which this aspect of Self communicates with the conscious mind is the same as how the 'subconscious' would but is somewhat more instinctive. The Hamingja does not care about the wellbeing of the rest of the Self per se; it cares only about survival. Exercise your will to perceive and remain in a passive, receptive state of mind. Impressions will come through, in the form of a sensation or knowing, or an emotion. If there are unresolved issues, you will perceive a sensation of rejection, or a sense of 'I don't like you'. This too counts as a perception; it could be anger, aggression and so forth. All these negative impressions indicate that there is something to fix in the relationship; doing so requires an exchange of emotion. You just need to ask the Hamingja why it feels that way and project a sense of confusion towards it.

Communication in words or logical thought is only for the conscious mind, as the Hamingja uses a form of pure thought or rather intent to communicate. The important part of the previous instruction was the sense of 'confusion', which will be the part received by the Hamingja. The sense of confusion will prompt it to send a new sensation or emotion towards your conscious mind, which you will need to interpret and put into context in your conscious mode of thinking.

Repeat this process until you have an idea of why it is feeling that way and then try to justify what has caused it by turning it into a new sensation you project back at it.

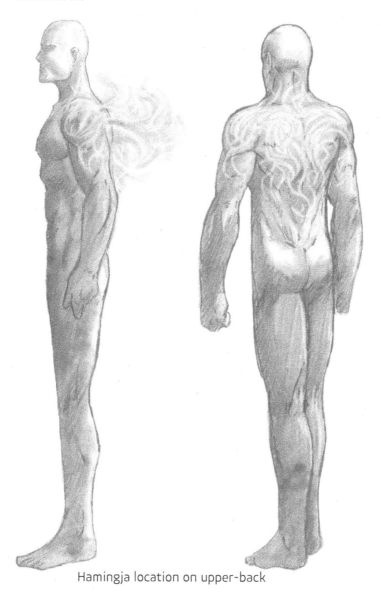

Hamingja location on upper-back

For instance, sometimes the Hamingja is angry because you did something harmful to it. If the reason for your action was that you had no choice because you lacked understanding of the situation, someone betrayed you and forced you to do something you did not want to or simply if you are sorry for that, project these impressions (or emotional senses) as you communicate with it. You will be amazed by just how much better you will start to feel once these nagging elements are resolved. Remember not to use just words, but attach the corresponding emotional or sensory response to these communications. As a matter of fact, words do not work, and we are so used to communicating in linguistic forms that we often forget that, in the grander scheme of things, language is a totally meaningless jumble of sounds. Words are empty (in most cases). 'Subconscious' elements of our selves do not recognise them in direct communications. Instead, in their attempts to do so, they will scan memories to identify what is related to the words, often with totally undesirable or unforeseeable results and misinterpretations.

Quick Steps

1   Relax and enter into a meditative state.
2   Feel the Hamingja as a patch of energy on the back in between your shoulder blades.
3   Focus in on it, feel it and let the intention to communicate with it arise.
4   Use the runes ᛗ Maður (Mannaz) ᚨ Óss (Ansuz) ᚠ Fé (Fehu)
5   As you bathe in these rune's energies, remain perceptive and watchful for any impulse from the Hamingja.

6   Take note of sensations, impressions, feelings
    and emotions as they stir.

7   Respond, if you feel the need to, by sending a
    response in terms of an emotional or sensory
    message (as in you might feel the need to twitch,
    move, feel irritated, or feel completely at ease
    and so forth).

Having started to smooth out the relationship
with the Hamingja, you are ready to focus on giving
it a workout. Using Galdr and uttering the ᚠ Fé (Fehu)
rune whilst manipulating its energy is the starting
point. This is what one can term the neutral energy
for the Hamingja, its default, then the life force and
then finally your personal energy, which is unique to
every individual.

Returning into a relaxed state, become aware of
sitting in the middle of an incredible expanse, literally
as if you were in the very middle of an infinite universe
with nothing in it other than your Self. Utter the ᚠ Fé
(Fehu) rune. Sit for a few moments hearing the sound
of the rune echoing in all that energy, feeling its heat
and enjoying its red colour. With a firm perception of
its energy, feel it as a prime runic energy. It is funda-
mentally linked to the first outpouring of Muspelheim,
the first event from which other life springs forth.
Let all this significance flow through the energy as a
sensation, as a fundamental meaning. Slowly shift
your awareness to the Hamingja on your back. Feel
its boundaries and be within it. From this state of
mind, focus on being within the Hamingja; with each
in-breath pull the fiery energies of ᚠ Fé (Fehu) into it.
More and more, repeat this process of concentrating
ᚠ Fé's (Fehu) energies into your Hamingja. Do so for

a count of three breaths, then refocus on the ᚠ Fé (Fehu) energies outside of yourself and will them to fade gradually until none are left in the vast space about you, but maintain the concentrated ᚠ Fé (Fehu) energy that is in your Hamingja!

Slowly come out of the trance, becoming aware of your physical environment once more. You should feel the location where the Hamingja is to be slightly heavier. It can at times feel odd or annoying. Simply allow these sensations to pass. In case there is any serious disturbance, use the rune ᛦ Ýr (Elhaz) to strengthen the walls of the Hamingja and your auric field (see chapter on protection, below).

Quick Steps

1   Enter into a relaxed state.

2   Visualise yourself sitting in the middle of an infinite empty universe.

3   Utter the rune ᚠ Fé (Fehu), hearing its name echoing throughout the universe, seeing the burning red energy flood everywhere and feeling the heat.

4   Shift your awareness into the Hamingja (thick energy patch on your back in between your shoulder blades).

5   From within the Hamingja, breathe in three breaths. As you do, visualise yourself breathing in not air but the fiery red burning energy of the rune, which is all around you.

6   Shift your focus on the infinitely filled space around you and will that energy to fade away. Preserve what you have inhaled into the Hamingja; do not allow that to fade.

7   Gradually return to normal awareness by re-
    focusing on your immediate environment and
    your physical body (Lik).

Practice each and every day. Increase the number
of breaths gradually by three, then six, then nine and
finally twelve, at which point stop increasing them
and instead make each breath deeper, pulling in more
and more energy and condensing it (but making sure
to avoid straining the breath while doing so).

At a certain point you will reach a cap, where taking
in any more energy will cause discomfort. This is the
indication that you have reached the current limit. It
will grow with practice; no need to push too far too
fast. The last thing you want is a fracturing of the
Hamingja. Having to overuse ᛦ Ýr (Elhaz) in this case
is a sign that you are overdoing it and risking damage.
Just slow down, take a day or two to relax and allow
the other parts of your Self to balance out. Knowing
one's limit is of vital importance in all this type of
work, no matter whether one is dealing with the
Hamingja, High Galdr, the Fylgja or any other aspects
thereof. Know your limits and push gently against
them, a little each time slowly and steadily until they
stretch and expand.

Here are some things you can keep an eye out
for: as the Megin increases, the first sign will be a
sense of wellness, of being alive. Gradually a feeling
of being re-energised will take hold and physical
health problems will smooth out. This is the first stage.
After each practice, you will perceive a gradual type
of sensation running about the surface of your skin.
It is odd and difficult to describe: cool yet not cold,
giving off an electric type of buzz but without being

electric at all. For those who are able to, they will notice a clear difference between Megin and the life force; they are essentially unmistakably different to the point where, having experienced Megin all over the body, it becomes impossible to ever confuse the two. The third sign of an increasing Megin pool and the quality of that pool is experiencing a sense of awe or something wonderful, which can be slightly intimidating to other people. A type of fearful or respectful distancing occurs from those who have interacted with the Megin, coupled with a distinct impression of difference that is 'subconsciously' perceived. It is very much like the "power of awfulness"[22] described by Marett when discussing the perceptibility of mana. These reactions are a good point to be aware of and to understand, but ultimately should be ignored as this reflects other people's reaction to the Megin. Eventually, as the spark of Self starts to change the Megin, a type of attraction develops as others respond to the 'sense of greatness' from within. In any case, the increasing Megin pool will not go unnoticed — it simply cannot be. With that in mind, you will need to deal with the problem of being noticed by predators.

HAMINGJA FOR PROTECTION

Protection is essential, especially in the early stages of development. It becomes important when you start to produce Megin, which is infused with your own individual Spark of Self's essence. Most people skip over protection but, in this case, it can be a critical mistake.

In this section, we will build upon those basics with a little adaptation for the work at hand. One should be well aware of the dangers of electromagnetic intrusions, especially in today's world of technology. You need to understand how those frequencies, even though invisible to the mundane human eye, pierce through the auric fields and cause micro-fractures in the Hamingja's 'skin'. This allows the energy robbers free reign into our pool of Megin. What they are and why they prey on humankind is of little relevance to us at this point. Frankly, what one needs to focus on is preserving our resources rather than letting something or someone else use them.

To that end, chant the rune ᛦ Ýr (Elhaz); see its golden light, freely flowing, shining all around you. Breathe it in, and pull it into the Hamingja patch located between your shoulder blades. Will it to radiate through the entire auric field, to radiate into and through you until all the universal energy of ᛦ Ýr (Elhaz) is radiating outwards like a golden sun. Wrap this golden energy about you as if it were a mantle and feel its boundaries grow firm and strong. Once done, maintain it in your mind.

The next step is to do the same with the rune ᚺ Hagall (Hagalaz). Feel its icy whiteness with a slight bluish tint energy leave a chill as it makes contact. Pull it all in and will it to reinstate the purity of your own energies. Next, do the same with ᚹ Vin (Wunjo). Feel its soft, cool, icy blues flow about and inhale these. As with the other two, wrap this energy about yourself, this time focusing on ᚹ Vin (Wunjo), establishing the inner harmony of your being and maintaining that harmony.

Quick Steps

1   Chant the rune ᛦ Ýr (Elhaz) and visualise its golden vibrant light flowing endlessly about you; feel its light touch, its soft yet firm embrace.

2   Shift your focus into the Hamingja (in between the shoulder blades on your upper back).

3   Breathe in the golden light; use however many breaths you feel you need, just avoid straining at any cost (maximum of nine breaths).

4   Feel the golden light and hear the name of the rune, glowing out of the Hamingja throughout the entire auric field. Will this golden light to wrap around your whole form and remain there,

strengthening you and pushing back any intrusions.

5   Repeat the same process using the H Hagall (Hagalaz) rune, feeling its icy touch and visualising it in a blue-ish white energy.

Enhanced Protective Field

6   Do the same with the ᛈ Vin (Wunjo) rune, visualising its energy in a light yet vibrant icy

blue, feeling its cold, comfortable touch and willing it to establish a state of harmony in all it makes contact with.

7   Finish the exercise by wrapping the energies around yourself and willing them to harmonise and purify all within the auric field.

8   Gradually return your focus to the physical and back to your daily life.

This will cause a protecting, balancing and harmonising pattern in the energy to form. Those who are balanced are, by virtue of their balance, protected. This is then further enhanced by the protective nature of Y Ýr (Elhaz), which has the secondary function of elevating the vibrational rate of that which it touches. This in and of itself will be protective. Rising sufficiently in vibrational frequency moves one up and beyond the reach of beings or things of a lower vibrational pattern, making you 'unreachable'. Those who are extremely high in terms of vibration become completely invisible to those of lower levels. In order for beings of lower vibration to see those of higher ones, they need to either meet on the physical level (face to face), or the being of a higher vibration needs to lower his / her vibrations down to the level of the lower one. The law of vibration applies universally to all of creation (including all human beings!).

In later practices when the Hamingja is personified, simply apply this practice in the same manner but wrap the energies around the form of the Hamingja and breathe the energy into its form rather than the physical body (Lik).

PERSONIFICATION OF THE HAMINGJA

Having achieved ample Megin and assured that the Hamingja is well protected, the stage for the critical part of this set of exercises has been reached. It is time to personify and shape it. This is the first stage of working with the core of the Self. At this point, mostly what is involved is becoming aware of the core's characteristics and power aspects. This is an important step in Self-knowing and will greatly enhance subsequent work with the personified Hamingja.

Start off by going into a reflective meditation, of which the sole and entire purpose is to listen to the mind within, to discern the heart's desires and any goals one's consciousness has. Many will start this practice by having a set of preconceived goals as to what they ultimately want to do, what they would like to become and in which energies they want to specialise. The vital part here is not to allow those things to colour one's perception. These can be added later on but should not determine the core being. That perception needs to be allowed to flow of its own will and the first thing that comes to mind should not be taken as being the core itself.

The main goal here is to dig deeply into yourself, see what resonates with the Self and look into the colours, sensations, emotions, bursts of meaning and so forth. Having gathered as many of these as possible, take each one in turn and let it be present in your thoughts. Ask, how does it make you feel? The answer to that question should provide the final guidance as to whether that concept, energy, thought, shape, etc. should or should not be included.

Having built the list of things to include, you are ready to undertake the next step, which involves spending a few days reflecting on the items in the list. At this time, you should try to identify the un-derlying energy type(s). This should result in a dominant one and several secondary ones. You can identify the dominant one based on how many of the items in the list are related to each other. Some might know what this underlying energy is, while others might get subtler hints pointing to it or even variations of it. Simply go with the process. It might be the energy of a rune, one of the elements, one of the worlds or even that of a God; just identify it. However, there are two energies it cannot be: the life or death force. Those are technically not energies, so if these pop up, they will have to be excluded from the list. Another of the things it cannot be is 'chaos'. What most un-derstand as chaos is simply an illusion in itself. Nor can it be evil or good; those do have energetic patterns but these are more akin to polarities of energy based on human interpretation rather than energetic types per se. Positive and negative are also unusable. These are but conceptions or polarities rather than energies. Light or dark, however, are perfectly valid since they are, technically speaking, energies too.

In any event, having to consider such abstract concepts will necessitate the personalisation of them. In other words, even if light is a common occurrence, it is impossible for a being incarnate to express the pure abstract light; rather, the personalised expression of light is in play. It is crucial to get to the bottom of what this personalised expression of it actually is. Having done so, it is the characteristics of light that are worked with rather than the archetypal version.

If an item on the list points to a God or Goddess, you will have to look at his or her energies and see what the entity's fundamental characteristics are and use those. However, do not use Oðin's energy; you are not part of Oðin nor would you want to be joined at the hip with a divinity and become totally dependent on them for anything you will ever do. It might seem like a good idea at one point, but in the long run, everyone has an Ørlög of his or her own to guide evolutionary living, while that of a divinity is counter-productive to the Self. If you do come up with the qualities of the God, look at what they are and think what energies would be corresponding to them, then just use those energies instead. This will allow the same energies with which you are resonating to express themselves in you in a unique way.

The next thing to do is to look at your Fylgja, assuming you have worked with it in the past. This will provide additional pointers as to the type of energies that have been embodying over multiple incarnations. Look at the animal shape; what does it convey? You should add these Fylgja energy patterns and if all is as it should be, they will be part of the core dominant ones. If they are not, you should carefully consider this fact: Is there a reason why? Are they being dismissed? Avoided? Are they instinctively being rejected? And if so, why? In case there is a disparity, you should deal with it before moving forward. Note that although the core energy cannot be changed, the secondary ones can be added to or even removed (albeit with difficulty for removal).

Quick Steps

1   Spend as much time as possible sitting in quiet solitude and turning your awareness within. Reflect on what makes you unique. What qualities are within your being? Break what is found into ideas, concepts, energies, thoughts, shapes, sensations, etc. and exclude the ones that you want or wish or desire strongly. Those are illusory; we only want what we do not know we have or what is external to our Self.

2   Having obtained a list, group the items into as many main categories as possible. You will notice commonalities, linked concepts and so forth. Such items are in fact different manifestations of the same quality of Self.

3   Next break down the list into primary and secondary characteristics. Then try to link those into specific energy types or groups, for instance, strength, determination, uplifting personality, supportive, organised, action driven and so forth. All these can also be linked into specific runic patterns. For instance, strength belongs to the ᚾ Úr (Uruz) rune, uplifting personality is a ᚹ Vin (Wunjo) characteristic, organised is a ᚱ Reið (Raidho) one and so on.

4   If you have worked with the Fylgja (Norse animal totem or spirit guide), add its qualities to the list. Those are part of you whether you like it or not.

5   Reflect on these qualities, and identify with them until you get a 'feel' for the Self. Remember to include any negative ones too! What you might consider negative could be a balancing necessity!

Having ironed out at least an idea of what the core dominant energy is, it is time to get down to some serious work! Time for a bit of activity!

This exercise is rather simple yet very complex in its execution, hence it is worth re-reading this procedure a few times until you have attained a firm grasp of the order of things.

Start by relaxing and letting go of the world; enter into a relaxed state of mind. Chant the rune ᛊ Sól (Sowilo), allowing its blinding light energy to flood your awareness and perceptions, feeling its all-penetrating light rays flow through your body energising it as it does. See the pure white electric sparks of its lightning quality flood the atmosphere. As your focus and senses become 'in-tune' with this runic energy, breathe it in. Inhale nine breaths, pulling all that electric light energy into your body; directing it into the blood stream should suffice. If this proves to create too much tension, stop at the point where the tension becomes more than simply noticeable. There is no point in overloading and harming the body; that is NOT the aim of this practice. As the rune's energy floods the blood stream, will it to activate the DNA within. Will it to awaken those parts that are still dormant and match the qualities of the core energies identified previously.

This is the key to the entire practice. This rune carries all the potential of the Self. It represents all manifestations of the Spark of Self and hence has the innate potential of awakening those parts of the Self no matter where it is directed. As its influence flows through the blood and the will to awaken the core energy is carried within it, those parts of the DNA that correspond to the expression of these qualities will gradually awaken and start vibrating. Whilst doing this part of the practice, it is vitally important to keep the characteristics of the Self identified in the previous meditation in mind. Otherwise, it will fail. An awakened mind directs the expression of the

Self via the DNA. Besides, what we are targeting here is the activation of abilities, in what sciences call the 'junk DNA', not other aspects of physiological DNA.

Quick Steps

1   Relax and allow the world around you to fade. Daydream for a few minutes to relax the mind and unwind the subconscious.

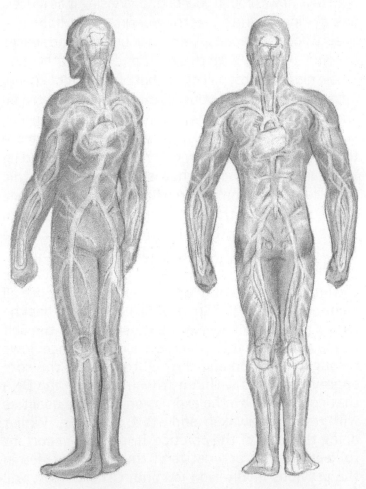

DNA charged megin flowing through bloodstream

2   Visualise yourself in the centre of an endless, empty universe.

3   Chant the rune ⚡ Sól (Sowilo). As you do, see it explode in electrifying light all around you. Now the endless emptiness is filled with the bright whiteness of the rune's energy.

4   As you breathe in, pull that energy into your body, into your blood stream, so that it floods everything and eventually concentrates in the DNA. The DNA is visualised as the double helix with small white electric sparks flowing through it. At the same time, you should focus on feeling all those characteristics of the Self identified in the previous exercise radiating out of the charged and glowing DNA.

5   Bathe in the activated DNA; feel it vibrating and emanating all those characteristics of Self previously identified. You might get a sense of an overflowing quality, which was dormant previously awakening now. Just take note of it and feel the harmony with the Self expressing itself through your DNA.

6   Rinse and repeat over the course of several days, weeks, months until you not only feel the vibration of personally charged DNA but can activate it at will.

Several sittings in this meditation might be required, but eventually the vibration of the DNA will be perceived, more so as a type of feeling that will expand into a specific sound. At this point, drive this sense of vibrational DNA throughout your whole body; identify with it completely until it echoes throughout your mind, feelings and body, allowing it to flood your auric field and personal energy.

Mastering this is important for many practical uses. In this context, the next step is to focus this vibrational energy of the DNA into the Hamingja on the back as would be done with the ᚠ Fé (Fehu) fires.

Quick Steps

1 Awaken the personal DNA as described above.
2 Feeling it vibrating and the energy pulsating with the characteristics of the Self, transfer your awareness into the Hamingja.
3 As you breathe in draw that DNA energy from the body into the Hamingja. Do this three times initially, increasing by one breath until you reach six.
4 Refocus on your body, and repeat the activating practice outlined previously BUT do not fill the Hamingja again (you have done so already; all you are doing is recharging the DNA).

Filling the Hamingja with such runic energy brings about a very distinct effect, which is best experienced rather than described. Repeat this type of charging at least three to six times before moving on to the final step.

Transfer your focus onto the Hamingja, which should be shining as it is charged with DNA energy. Maintaining your focus is essential. Once you are done focusing on the Hamingja, will it to expand; it will use the DNA energy to fuel its expansion. The expansion will feel as if it is a type of cool, gel-like substance; allow it to grow and take the shape of the body. This identical shape of the body and the Hamingja establishes a resonance with the energy body (Hamr), physical body (Lik) and Hamingja. Having adopted the relevant form, experience the DNA energy flowing through it, bathing it from the inside out. Do note that some clothing will take form automatically without any involvement of the conscious or will. These are symbolic representations of your core's energies OR patterns, and should be preserved without interference. During this practice, the mind is looking at the world around you from WITHIN the Hamingja, which is being shaped, and it should be kept there; do not allow it to switch back to the perspective of the physical body (Lik). If it does, immediately refocus until the point of consciousness is back within the Hamingja, not the body.

It is important to note that when working with the DNA energy and infusing it with ⚡ Sól's (Sowilo) runic energy, it will cause a shift in those energies. It is vital not to interfere with that. No being living in Midgard can express the full purity of light of ⚡ Sól (Sowilo), irrespective of what it is or is believed to be. Midgard incarnation will cause everyone to be influenced by all Nine World's energies, albeit to different degrees, but they will all exert an influence. Adding the personal energy will also cause it to shift. It should come as no surprise when its white electric properties change into something else entirely. That is a result of the expression of the Self's characteristics and patterns combined with various degrees of each of the Nine World's patterns. Even beings of pure light cannot incarnate in Midgard and express pure light with one exception, that being Baldur himself or his Hamingja. It is critical to take note of what the resultant energy and its patterns feel like, look like and sound like. These will all be facets of the personal core energy and recalling those will allow quick activation of the Self without having to repeat this entire practice each time (once you have fully mastered it, of course).

Once you have established a solid shape with the relevant details, use the rune ᛒ Bjarkan (Berkano), then ᚠ Fé (Fehu). Having uttered these runes, as their energies flow, focus on the shapes of the runes themselves as they radiate their energies around the body, then move them (by breathing or directing them mentally) into the personified Hamingja. It is important to do so whilst remaining within the personified Hamingja (not the physical body(Lik)). This is an important matter of focus and perspective. As they enter, feel their characteristics and powers, and breathe in their emitted universal energy into the newly formed Hamingja until you have reached three breaths. Will their power to solidify the form (ᛒ Bjarkan (Berkano) will do that) and to empower it (ᚠ Fé (Fehu) will do that part).

Allow the rest of the universal flow of these two runes to fade away until they are no longer present. From within the Hamingja, step back into the physical body (Lik), merging with it. Allow for a couple of minutes to ground and get back to ordinary consciousness.

Quick Steps

1   Start by relaxing and allowing the world around you to fade from awareness.

2   Follow the instruction in the previous exercise to charge up your Hamingja, then refocus on the physical body (Lik). It should be shining with DNA-charged energy.

3   Spend a few minutes refocusing on the Hamingja and will it to expand. It will use the DNA energy you have charged it up with to fuel this expansion. Keep expanding it until it is an exact replica of your physical body (Lik).

4   Keep your awareness within the newly formed

Hamingja, but focus on the energy within it; feel it, experience it, enjoy it. It is the DNA energy, your primary qualities powered and flowing through it.

5 Look around from inside the Hamingja's perspective, and feel its form.

6 Having gained a solid footing in its form, from within it, chant the rune ᛒ Bjarkan (Berkano) then ᚠ Fé (Fehu). Feel and enjoy their energies around your Hamingja's form as they gently radiate.

7 Breathe from within the Hamingja's form. As you do, inhale the rune's energies, for a set of three breaths each.

8 Feel the form solidify, then be empowered.

9 Next simply step back into the physical body (Lik), feeling it pull you in through your back as your awareness clicks back into physical focus.

This brings the practice to an end. On the following day, simply go back into a slight relaxed state and focus on the form of the Hamingja as if it were standing stuck on your back. Shift the mental focus into it and step back slightly out of sync with the physical body (Lik). Then use the rune ᚠ Fé (Fehu) and breathe in six breaths directly into the personified Hamingja. Step back into the physical body (Lik) and return to normal consciousness.

Repeat until you have reached nine breaths, every time stepping out of and then back into the physical body (Lik). Having reached nine breaths, switch to ᛉ Ýr (Elhaz) until you have completed six breaths. Following this, the Hamingja is filled on a daily basis with generic life force then with ᚠ Fé (Fehu) runic energy by no more than three breaths of each. Having done so for nine days, it is permissible to move onto the next set of practices.

Quick Steps

1   Relax a little, then feel yourself stepping out of the physical, inside the Hamingja and stand straight behind the physical.

2   Chant the rune ᚠ Fé (Fehu) and breathe in up to six breaths, inhaling the fiery hot energy (make sure you inhale into the Hamingja, not the physical body (Lik)).

3   Step back into the physical and allow it to pull you and the Hamingja back in.

4   Repeat, increasing by one breath every day until you reach nine.

5   Then do the same with the ᛦ Ýr (Elhaz) rune, starting at six and working up to nine by a daily increase of one.

6   Having done so, if you have mastered the life force, you can proceed to breathing that into the Hamingja, following it with three breaths of the ᚠ Fé (Fehu) rune's energy; if not, skip this step.

7   Each time, make sure you re-merge with the physical body (Lik) and return to daily awareness. You should not have any Hamingja-driven perceptions whatsoever at any point!

A couple of notes before moving on. This is the stage where the need to be careful arises. If at any time the Hamingja tries to walk out without being consciously directed, pull it back in immediately. This should be a totally non-negotiable point. If it starts to be aggressive towards you, pull it back in instantly and avoid working with it for several days. Simply pull it back in and ignore it. After that, communicate with it, and see what caused it to react that way. Use the same method as outlined at the outset (that of emotional sensory feedback). Keep in mind, just because it is in humanoid form does not mean it communicates as a human, nor does it mean it acts as one either. It is still and always will be an aspect of the 'subconscious' instinctive Self. You should remember this when using it. Be aware that threatening it, or being aggressive towards it will not work and will be counter-productive. Remember, it is the source of all Megin, hence it will always have the upper hand in any confrontation with the rest of your Self other than the Megin-fuelled breath (Önd). Dealing with issues in a responsible manner is the key, not force, threatening or imposing one's will. Listen to it, make it a part of your daily life and it will respond in kind. Work with it and it will work with you; it is, after all, a part, an aspect, of yourself!

Awakening the Core of the Self

This is where things start to get exciting! At this point, the core dominant energy starts to be the dominant energy used to fill the Hamingja. This will produce a specific type of Megin, which is unique to the Self as an individuated being. It is the ᛗ Maður (Mannaz) imprint of the Megin, which only you can produce. This special type of Megin is unique in creation; no other being will have the same type. It is a direct expression of the natural and 'supernatural' (in fact there is no such thing as 'supernatural', just aspects of the natural that are not understood / or yet discovered) part of your Self. When working with this type of Megin and producing greater and greater quantities of it, a special ability is unlocked. This is best thought of as spontaneous event causation according to the individual will. Simply willing something to happen (providing one has the sufficient amount of this 'individualised' Megin) will cause it to take place. The more Megin available to spare, the faster events manifest.

Even though this might all seem wonderful, and in some ways it is, it does have an important down side as well: joking about things will have to be avoided at all costs, as will lying and deceit. Why? Because thoughts about something can unleash that into reality. In other words, telling a small lie such as not being able to make it into work for a day due to being 'sick' might have been a harmless thing to occasionally do before. At this point, however, such a thing will cause such an illness to manifest within a very short time (and for some it can virtually be that same day). In English, there is a good luck saying, which is 'break a leg'; it is a social linguistic play on words. However, for someone with this level of Megin, this expression would result in the person to whom these words are said to actually break their leg. This is a good example of a completely innocent set of words with a humorous intent, which actually causes great harm. Wishing strangers 'good luck' is also to be avoided at all cost because it will spill some personal Megin over to them in order to bring forth that good luck.

Being aware of what one does, one says and one thinks as well as what one feels at all times is a fundamental basis of living in the NOW. In this case, it is an essential component of staying safe and keeping the Megin pool charged.

A point to note is that, having started working with individualised Megin, the reserves of Megin should never, ever, EVER be allowed to drop too low. Why? Because being supercharged with unique Megin causes all seen and unseen beings to perceive it like a glowing sun in a dark universe; its amplification will by its very nature attract them like flies. Having a strong Hamingja with a fully charged pool of Megin stops them from being able to cause harm or drainage. However, allowing it to become empty gives rise to vulnerability. This is an effect of the strength of charge and does not require any additional work other than keeping the charge full.

Start by sitting in a relaxed position and sinking into a relaxed state of mind. Letting go of everything, allow the world to gradually fade away as the state of trance is induced.

Utter the following runes in this order: Sól, Perð, Fé, Þurs, Óss, Hagall, Maður, Óðal, Sól (for those of you using the Germanic names, the equivalents are: Sowilo, Perthu, Fehu, Thurisaz, Ansuz, Hagalaz, Mannaz, Othala, Sowilo), allowing their energies to flood the universe with you at its centre. With these runes use the traditional red colours unless you are using High Galdr.

ᛋᚲᚠᚦᚠᚺᛘᛟᛋ

Having done so, relax and bathe in their energy, sound and vibration. What this runic chant does is to echo the experiences and potential of the Self stepping out of the Ginnungagap into individuation. Further information about this runic pattern will be given in a later publication in order to avoid getting off course herein.

Shift the focus into the personified Hamingja. Do not lose the awareness of the runic energies, you have just called forth as you shift focus. Either breathe in that energy from the Hamingja or simply use your will to pull as much of it as possible without straining. Once the Hamingja's form is vibrating with this energy and no more can be taken in with-out strain, allow the runic energy to fade from the OUTSIDE holding onto the energy inside of the Hamingja. Give it a few minutes to allow it to adapt to the energetic flow. Typically, you will feel a distinct energy rush; if not, you will sense a type of tension. Whichever it is, simply allow it to pass. Taking a few minutes for keeping still and enjoying this rush is a more than acceptable way to deal with integrating the new flow into the emerging Hamingja.

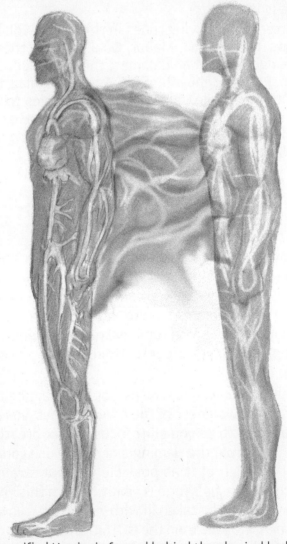

Personified Hamingja formed behind the physical body (Lik)

Once this newfound tension / rush has calmed down, allow all the energies to fade from your awareness (both within the Hamingja and within the universe at large). Next, utter the rune ᚠ Fé (Fehu) directly within the Hamingja, feeling the burning rush of runic power only inside its form. This will cause a special type of Megin to be produced. This version of Megin will not have the cool sensations of typical Megin, instead it will feel very unusual, a flowing, all-pervasive watery type. Enjoy the sensation; it is unique to this runic chant and only used in conjunction with it. As this Megin flows through the (personified) Hamingja, allow it to flow outwards and wrap it around yourself so that it resembles an auric field. Here again, allow the sensation(s) to pass after having acknowledged or enjoyed them and observe the rune's energy fade away as well.

Quick Steps

1 Relax and allow the immediate surroundings and world to fade from awareness.

2 Visualise yourself sitting in a vast, empty space.

3 Chant the following runes (in this precise order): ᛋᚲᚠᚦᚱᚺᛗᛜᛋ and allow their energy to flood the space all around you (see Appendix A for correspondences).

4 Feel the energy, bathe in it, sense how it is a manifestation of the Self stepping out of the Great Nothingness and becoming something: that individualised something that ultimately down the generational lines produced you.

5 Transfer your awareness into the Hamingja by stepping into it and out of the physical body (Lik); stand behind it.

6 Either breathe into or pull into the Hamingja as much of this runic energy combination as you can without feeling any strain. Then allow whatever remains without to fade away (but not that which you have inside of it).

7 You should feel a rush; enjoy it and then allow it to naturally fade (without interfering with it).

8 Finally, from within the Hamingja chant the ᚠ Fé (Fehu) rune, feeling its burning rush and tension radiate from the centre of the Hamingja outwards.

9 Step back into the physical body (Lik), and allow it to pull the Hamingja form and your awareness back into their respective places.

You have two choices: one is to simply step back into the physical body (Lik) and re-merge the personified Hamingja with it. The other is to use inner High Galdr and utter ᚠ Fé (Fehu) (only once) and then re-merge into the physical body (Lik). The former will allow your Hamingja in its own time to generate the Megin. In the latter case, it will force production to start immediately. If you use the latter approach, make sure you do not do any other Galdr (or meditation); simply focus on mundane tasks for the next few hours. You need to allow time to pass in order for the generation of Megin to take place uninterrupted.

This practice might seem complicated and intricate but do not allow this to dissuade you; with practice, it can take only a few minutes to perform effectively. It is essentially simple once you get into the flow. It is a little more complex than the others since you are working in the realm of the Ásgarðians, specifically using techniques from Húnir (in other words, higher consciousness way of doing things). It can be rather tricky when consciousness is not functioning at that level, yet. Nonetheless, patience and practice will not only allow you to perform this within a few minutes, but doing so will start elevating your consciousness to that higher level. This practice combines a multitude of goals with one single practice: reaching higher consciousness, enhancing the Hamingja, expanding its capabilities, generating individualised Megin and developing the abilities for the instant casting of will into the worlds.

CONSCIOUSLY CONTROLLING THE PERSONIFIED HAMINGJA

This practice is somewhat tricky, not in terms of difficulty but in terms of getting it to 'click into place'. What we mean is that it can take time for consciousness to slip fully into the personified Hamingja. It is important to make one point from the outset here: the goal is not a complete transfer of conscious awareness, instead it is to achieve a type of dual function of the conscious mind. We seek to reach the point where acting consciously from within the personified Hamingja AND the physical body (Lik) simultaneously is possible, not full projection of conscious awareness into the Hamingja. On its own, it cannot sustain that.

The important factors to keep in mind when practicing this are the following: the stronger the relationship with the Hamingja the easier it will be; being in a state of dual consciousness will cause rapid mental fatigue. This is one of those things that become easier to sustain over time. If consciousness is lost whilst within the Hamingja's form, immediately upon regaining consciousness pull the Hamingja back into the physical body (Lik) re-merge into it and take a break. Remember, Megin is used to fuel this dual-conscious state; recharge often! Avoid forcing things. There will be hurdles, there will be tricky parts and there will be obstacles. At such times, uttering ᛏ Nauð (Nauthiz) and ᛗ Maður (Mannaz) runes and bathing in their energy will help you get through any especially difficult patches. At all costs, avoid forcing results; doing so is ultimately counterproductive and will cause friction between the conscious will and the Hamingja. Remember, the 'subconscious' mind will be adapting to the work at hand but in its own time and in its own manner. If forced to do things, it will rebel and a rebellious 'subconscious' is the mightiest of ALL foes.

As usual, sit in a comfortable position and relax. Allow the world to fade from your mind. Moving into a relaxed state of mind, allow the relaxation of body and awareness to take place. When ready, will the personified Hamingja to step out of the physical body (Lik) and stand behind it (this should be a very familiar state by now).

Focusing on the Hamingja, shift the awareness into it. As much as possible, feel yourself inside of it; use its hands to brush against its form, feel its skin, let the senses sink into all the sensations it has to offer. Literally lose yourself in it. Follow through with this until the senses are firmly rooted within it. Try to see and hear from within it; hearing and seeing should be such that the input comes into the Hamingja's eyes and ears rather than directly into the mind (this helps avoid imagining things rather than seeing them), or from the physical senses. It will take a few sessions of repeating this practice until the sensory switch fully takes.

Quick Steps

1 Relax and let the world around you fade from awareness.

2 Shift your awareness into the Hamingja as you step out of the physical body (Lik) and stand behind it.

3 Next you will have to focus the sensory perceptions into the Hamingja's form.

4 Start by feeling its subtle energetic skin; become aware of those Megin-formed hands, using those hands to touch the Hamingja's form. Run them along it, feel its texture, allow your 'subconscious' mind to learn its shape, its sensations and so on.

5 Try to hear from the ears of the Hamingja's form, see from its eyes, smell from the nose and so forth. The aim is to sense from it rather than the physical body (Lik).

6 Once you have established a solid sensing from within the Hamingja, use its hands to touch your physical body (Lik). Here you will start by touching your back. Pay close attention; this is where confusion regarding your mental perceptions is highly likely to occur. Your mind will get 'muddled' as to whether it is the sense of feeling from the physical body (Lik) or the Hamingja that is driving the sensory input. It is very important to ensure that you iron out mentally the flow of touch that comes from the hands of the Hamingja and is received from the skin of the back of the physical body (Lik).

7 Rinse and repeat this mastering of sensory input. It is a very important skill to gain and is critical for more advanced work.

8 Upon completion of each practice session, simply

take a step forward within the Hamingja until it merges into the physical body (Lik) and return to daily awareness. This is important!

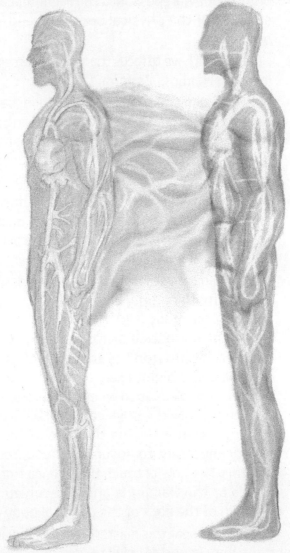

Personalised Hamingja solidifying by sensory transfer

Having achieved a sensory shift into the Hamingja and feeling its form, the next step is to move from within it. The first task is to use its hands to touch the physical back (this is familiar territory for the Hamingja, yet for the conscious mind, it is not so. Hence the sensory flow is from 'subconscious' to conscious rather than the usual inverse flow). This will cause a very odd sensory loop where the back or rather sensation of touching it comes from the hands of the Hamingja's sensory input AND from the physical body's (Lik) skin as it is touched. Once that perception is gained, use the conscious mind to split it so that it becomes clear which is flowing in from the Hamingja and which is from the physical body (Lik) (getting a good grip of this is the key to dual consciousness). Practice as many times as needed!

The next step is to walk in the Hamingja; remember not to get too far from the physical body (Lik) at first. The Hamingja is not a fully-fledged separate body that can host active consciousness independently of the other parts of the psycho-spiritual Self. Move too far and you run the risk of losing awareness with the Hamingja, allowing it to go loose somewhere, until it returns naturally . . . this is not ideal. Practice as many times as needed! Here, the key is to take one step out, then return, then take another, then another and so forth. This causes a stretching of the 'link' connecting the Hamingja to the rest of the Self through the physical body (Lik).

Quick Steps
1   Relax and shift your conscious awareness into the Hamingja.
2   As you step out of the physical body, stand in the

Hamingja and re-establish the sensory input from within it.

3 Once you are comfortable being in the Hamingja's form, take a step in it away from the physical body (Lik). This will cause a shift in spatial perception and might give rise to a sense of confusion or even panic. Should this occur, relax, re-focus and remain within the Hamingja.

4 Next, take another step away, then another until you are about an arm's length from the physical body (Lik). You will notice the auric field being stretched across the two forms. This is normal. Get familiar with this state and gradually reverse the steps until finally remerging into the physical body (Lik).

5 Return to physical awareness and end the practice for the day.

6 NEVER EVER EVER distance too far from the physical body (Lik); a couple of steps are the most the Hamingja can be separated from a living body, or the auric field will end up with a permanent tear, which can be very damaging. You have been warned. This is not something to be adventurous with; other parts of the psycho-spiritual Self construct are used for full separation, NOT the Hamingja.

7 The final step is to achieve the skill of moving in the Hamingja at the SAME time as the physical body (Lik), in effect being dually aware with the personified Hamingja walking behind the physical body (Lik), then progressing in this skill until you are able to do something that does not mimic the physical body's (Lik) movements or actions. Practice as many times as needed!

This practice has quite a few progressive stages. Between each session, remember to move the personified Hamingja out through the back and make it re-merge into the physical body (Lik) each time!

Quick Steps

1 Step out of the physical body (Lik) in your Hamingja form.

2 This time the task at hand is to not only establish the sensory focus within the Hamingja's form but also to keep a firm grip on sensory input from the physical. This will be tricky as you will be dealing with dual input simultaneously.

3 Having gained some proficiency in this, the next step is to work on moving both of those bodies at the same time. Simply have the Hamingja just behind the physical body (Lik) and move them both in sync.

4 Once you have achieved synchronous movement, it is time to try different movements and tasks in each. Please remember to do this in a safe place; it can get confusing at first and there is absolutely no reason to put yourself or anyone else at risk. Move away all dangerous/sharp objects, all things you could trip over and so forth. Then practice. Stick to simple things and work up to more complex ones. Remember to keep the Hamingja's form always close to the physical body (Lik) to avoid ripping your auric field permanently.

5 This practice should be considered mastered when you are able to walk behind your physical body (Lik) and observe from a different point of view, do runic chants whilst walking in physical

and so forth. Also remember the Hamingja has extended perceptions. In other words, it perceives the non-physical and the physical. What you are doing is expanding both conscious awareness and your perceptual apparatus.

6   When done, simply allow the Hamingja to re-merge into your physical body (Lik) by stepping into it from the back! (Not anywhere else; always use the back as the exit/entry point).

As your practice advances, you will no longer have a need to get into the relaxed states of mind to step into the Hamingja. A simple act of will is all that is required to split and gain conscious focus within it, virtually in a single instant. This is not necessary but is a nice ability to have in case of emergencies, especially when dealing with casting High Galdr from within the Hamingja. One could be in the middle of a conversation with someone and casting Galdr simultaneously or be in a meeting and fending off something that is trying to sap you (the amount of spiritual nonsense taking place in corporate board meetings is simply mind-blowing!). Gaining a good foothold in the Hamingja allows for a direct call to be made out to the Æsir or Vanir; doing so is pretty much like unleashing a radio frequency fuelled by Megin.

The lack of this knowledge is what prevents effective communication with Ásgarð. The specific practice will be revealed in full in subsequent work but it does required mastery of this first!

AWAKENING THE BREATH OF OÐIN

This part of the practices is very exciting. It takes the theories and practical work of the Norse Self to a whole new level. Here is where we encounter the domain of Lóðurr's gift. Lóðurr, generally speaking, does not like being the centre of attention; he is the silent one (for good reason). All he asks in return for the knowledge given is to have it pointed out that he is neither Loki nor Freyr. Having fulfilled the promise to do so, it is time to focus on the practice at hand.

In this practice, we are going to be blending the personalised Hamingja with the physical body (Lik), whilst preserving a state of semi-independence in both. It is a very different practice from simply re-merging the Hamingja into the physical body (Lik). This has two direct effects: the first is to cause a permanent stretching of the Hamingja. It gains a solid elasticity hence increasing the capacity for Megin storage and energy accumulation to what one can be forgiven for labelling a 'ridiculous' level. Second, it will cause the physical body (Lik) to be flooded with pure individualised Megin. Imagine the boundary between the physical body (Lik) and the Hamingja blurring, where the blood of the physical merges with the Megin of the Hamingja. This causes the gifts of Lóðurr to awaken and activate.

Additionally, doing this will initiate a merging of the active 'subconscious' with conscious awareness. Senses become hyperactive, expanding your ability to sense a wider range of impressions than ever before. This involves a gradually and steadily awakening of the clair-senses or more, accurately termed 'actual senses' rather than the restricted illusory ones that come as a default. As the Megin flows through the blood, it will activate the DNA; well, those parts of it that deal with the spiritual Self. You will notice 'your self' becoming more like the Self; expressing its actual nature will become second nature. The collective, the crowd and the masses will become more and more distant, and a gradual awakening of the Divine Self takes place. This practice is all about preparing the foundations for the full integration of all the parts of the Self into one uniform Divine Self.

Start by relaxing and going into a relaxed state of mind. Once relaxed, allow the world to fade out of your mind and into insignificance. Utter the rune ᚠ Óss (Ansuz). Allow its energy to flow through your body. Feel its vibrational power raising your consciousness and shifting it into a slightly ecstatic state, free from restriction, flowing, expanding and unlimited. Once you have reached that sensation of runic power, will it to fade completely.

Will the personified Hamingja to step out, with your awareness within it already. At this point, it will be like stepping out of your body yet still being within it. This automatic switch into dual-consciousness should require nothing more than a willed intent to achieve (providing your practice has been diligent up

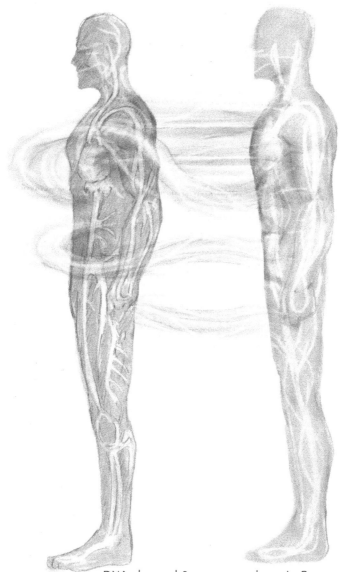

DNA charged & empowered megin flow
Hamingja to body and vice versa

to this point). Focus in on the Hamingja and allow the
sensory perceptions from it to flow; feel its form and

its energies. Having done so, touch the physical body (Lik) and feel it as an external touch of the physical body's (Lik) perspective. Slowly and gradually, move in such a manner as to blend into the physical body (Lik). What is meant here is that the physical hands and arms will blend with the Hamingja's hands and arms, while the legs will be fused with the physical legs and so forth. The essential point is that the arms overlap with the arms, the legs with the legs, the torso with the torso, etc. If the one is slightly larger than the other, that is not a problem. Keep the awareness of both the Hamingja AND the physical separate; in this practice, the one does not fuse into the other; they are kept distinct but overlap. Your awareness should be of both forms simultaneously. This can be very confusing to begin with as the senses and the mind will become horribly muddled as to where each is functioning or perceiving from. Just relax and allow the temporary confusion to pass, keeping in mind that each of these forms is a source of sensory information distinct and separate yet inter-connected.

Once that has settled down, feel the surface of your physical skin. It should be easy to notice the Megin flowing all over it (as the Hamingja is now expanded all over it). Will this Megin to fuse with the physical blood and flow through it. At the same time, will that Megin to activate your DNA and energise it, as it flows through the blood. Relax and observe. It is impossible to describe the sensations or experiences this produces since they will be dictated by the DNA and by the individualised Megin. Whatever they are, relax and maintain the point of view of an observer taking notes but not reacting to them (or the trance can break). As the DNA activates it creates an odd pulse. When this happens, will the pulse (and attached energy) to flow through the Megin back into the Hamingja. This causes a feedback loop. In the first part, when the Megin flooded the blood, the Hamingja's essence flooded the physical. With the DNA's pulse, the reverse is taking place and the essence of the physical is flooding the Hamingja. This will bring the two systems into a harmonic state and spill over characteristics from the one into the other. Most importantly, this action will give the Hamingja a certain elasticity, and the physical body (Lik) as a container will help 'solidify' the Hamingja. This is an essential step for preparing it as a vehicle of Divine essence and consciousness.

To end the practice, simply focus on the Hamingja and will it to fuse with the physical body (Lik) as in previous practices.

Quick Steps

1   Start by relaxing and allowing the world to fade from your awareness.

2   Chant the rune ᚠ Óss (Ansuz); as you do so, feel the dark blue airy energy flow through your body, mind and awareness. Flow with it. If done correctly, a sense of freedom should gradually build up to the point where it gives rise to a thrill of the mind, an excitement, a form of ecstasy.

3   Step out of the physical body (Lik) in your Hamingja. Remember to shift your awareness into it until your sensory perceptions flow from it.

4   With the Hamingja's hands, touch the physical body (Lik). This time, allow the Hamingja hands to blend into the physical hands. Make sure you keep them separate; do not allow them to fuse into each other; instead, they should overlap while occupying the same space.

5   Keep making the two overlap into each other, Hamingja legs over physical legs, torso over torso and so forth until both forms are occupying the same space and overlapping. Since the Hamingja is energetic, it will flow a little further than the physical. It shimmers with an electric type of blue glow, which can stretch up to half an inch above the skin. In Jarls, it will be much more dominant.

6   Keep awareness, sensory input and consciousness separate; the training with receiving input from the two simultaneously yet remaining distinct was preparation for this. Keep each one separate even when they occupy the same space.

7   From the Hamingja, feel the surface of your skin on the physical body (Lik), then feel the skin from the physical body's (Lik) point of view. Notice the distinct sensation of Megin and remember it.

8   Will the Megin to flood the blood stream (in the physical), fusing with it. Feel it, energise it and enliven it. As it does so, direct it to activate the DNA in your blood. If it helps, visualise and feel the double helix being flooded with the sparks of Megin, activating, enlivening and infusing. Take note of sensations, notice the individualised energy and qualities from previous practices surface and vibrate through the bloodstream. This will create an odd pulse from the DNA throughout the blood. Take note.

9   Allow this pulse to strengthen. As it does, it emits the pulse into the flow of Megin in the streams of the Hamingja (equivalent to blood capillaries, arteries and veins).

10 The flow of Megin should be from the Hamingja into the physical body's (Lik) blood, activating

the DNA, which pulses personalised Megin back into the Megin streams and Hamingja, harmonising the two and synchronising the flow of Self from the one to the other.

11 Repeat as many times as needed, until you are able to circulate and activate this synchronicity at will.

12 End the practice by merging the Hamingja's form into the physical body (Lik) by first separating from it, then merging in through the back as usual. Rinse and repeat this part until you can perform it without much effort.

The second stage is to get the core of the Self involved. Now the interesting part begins! Focus on your core (in the physical body (Lik)). Deep inside the solar plexus, sink until you reach centrality. This can be described as a sinking into the solar plexus, at a constant and flowing rate. The sinking produces a very deep true trance state, and you need to be skilled at maintaining your functioning awareness of the physical body (Lik) whilst sinking into the core, which takes place. Practice as much as necessary. At one point during this sinking, something 'clicks' and you will encounter a clear feeling of all those characteristics of the core energy and Self previously identified. At the core they can be described as pouring out of the 'sphere of the core' in the purest and subtlest manifestation. Having experienced this, the core Self has been touched; focus on it and will a merging (and sinking) of the conscious awareness into it. This is the Divine part of the Self; working with this will be covered in more detail later for it allows the full expression of the 'God is within' mystery and the whole concept of the physical body (Lik) being a Temple to be brought into actuality.

For now, whilst maintaining awareness of the core and hence Spirit part of the Self, the physical body (Lik) AND the form of the Hamingja, will the Megin to spill from the Hamingja, through the blood and DNA, into the solar plexus and sink through it into the spirit realm of the Self until it reaches the core. This triple state of awareness is tricky to gain and even more difficult to maintain; do not rush it, be patient. Practice until it all 'clicks' into place. A quick note: once the core Self is reached, providing the DNA and blood have been charged with Megin, the space around the core will pulsate with the individualised Megin. All that is needed is to pull it into the core itself. These perceptions, as well as the ability to maintain multi-levelled conscious awareness take time. Do not despair; persistence pays off incredibly well here and results will come to those who put the effort in. It is also an excellent way to train the will!

Once the Megin starts flowing into the core, the Divine Spark at the very centre of the core will start to awaken and activate. It will become fierier and more dynamic (all Divine Sparks are fire based, no exception anywhere in creation; however, what they radiate is unique to each one of us). As it activates it will pulsate energy rays as would a sun. Direct that out of the higher spirit realms via your solar plexus through the body and into the Hamingja. In case of difficulty here, simply switch the focus to the physical body (Lik) and feel those rays pulsating through the solar plexus whilst preserving awareness in the core and willing it to push the energy out through the solar plexus. Here, you are using the quantum point of the Self and, by acts of interaction, reshaping it and making it flow through the physical body (Lik). Those who are familiar with quantum physics will understand the concepts and probably be very surprised that they apply to the Self within!

Quick Steps

1 Relax and let go of your immediate surroundings.

2 Focus on your physical body (Lik), feel it, relax it. Shift your awareness to the midriff section of your body (commonly known as the solar plexus). It is an important intersection point for a multitude of nerve networks. In men, it is an even more important point because it is the central point of gravity of the physical form, hence also the central point of one's entire Self.

3 Visualise yourself inside that point, see, feel and sense from that point outwards. Once settled in that point, sink and allow yourself to go deeper and deeper. Keep on sinking. This will produce a deep trance. Keep on sinking, deeper and deeper until you feel a type of 'click'. It should be either proceeded or followed by a strong sense of the qualities of your Self (as identified in the previous work).

4 Sink into this sense of characteristics as they radiate outward. You will find yourself in the centre of the Self. Feel it radiating the characteristics of YOUR Self; sense it, get to know it.

5 Maintaining focus inside your core, expand your awareness so that you also become aware of your physical body (Lik), then add to that an awareness of the Hamingja as it overlaps the physical. Spend a couple of minutes strengthening and re-establishing this triple synchronous awareness. Having gained a firm grip of this three-fold awareness, expand the physical to include

not only the Hamingja but also the Megin flowing through it. Then, will it to flow into the physical blood and DNA. Remember to keep the threefold awareness; you MUST not lose focus of all that whilst expanding into the blood, DNA and Megin.

6 As the DNA gets activated with Megin and starts to pulse, feel it growing stronger and stronger until its pulse flows back through the physical body (Lik) into the space where the Spark of Self is. Let the pulse flow inwards towards you as you are in the centre of the Spark of Self. As it touches the spark, pull it in; if it helps, see yourself 'breathing' in that pulse's energy.

7 As this energy enters the Spark of Self, it will burst into hyperactivity and start to radiate out in a series of Megin-charged pulses of Self. These will be noticeably different from the previous one. How so depends entirely on your Self, making it impossible to describe.

8 As it pulses outwards, it will flow out of the solar plexus then throughout your physical body (Lik), back through the bloodstream into the Hamingja.

9 This completes one breath. Increase by one breath each time you want to increase the effects of this practice. At three complete breath cycles, you will be ready to move on. To end this, simply re-merge the Hamingja form with the physical body (Lik) and return to your daily life.

Having made this energy actually flow from the outer into the inner and then from the inner into the outer (blood and DNA into the core and then from the core back out through the solar plexus into the blood and DNA, then spill into the Megin in the Hamingja), you will notice a very empowering and distinctive effect, which will become obvious to the whole totality of your Being. Details are unnecessary here; results speak for themselves. All that is worth saying is that the Divine Self surfaces into the world and in each and every one of these breaths and subsequent actions. In other words, the Megin-fulled breath (Önd) starts to flow. Blessed be the Breath of Oðin within!

This is what the Breath of Oðin actually is; the flow of Megin, personalised by the DNA and the Self's core, flowing through the physical, Hamingja and spirit of the individual. It is both the flow and what flows, the substance and the function (in other words the characteristics of this energy combined with its power set in motion during an in-flow and out-flow motion). It is also at times referred to as: Megin-fuelled or Megin-filled breath.

Regardless how long it takes to master this practice, it is damn well worth doing until you have fully mastered it. It is the second step to fully awakening the divine within. If you look back over the practices so far, you will notice that the Hamingja has now awoken and become active; the DNA is activated and individualised Megin flows through the two and the physical body (Lik), which subsequently flows into the core of the Self. The core pulses out the Breath of Oðin, which in turn flows from that most mysterious place in the spirit realm of the Self back through the physical body (Lik) merging with the Megin and empowering the Hamingja. The final piece of the puzzle to a fully awoken Divine consciousness is the addition of the merging of the geometric (or animal–human formed) Fylgja, for which this is the preparatory process.

Keep increasing the individualised Megin, keep working on making it flow through the physical body (Lik) into the core Self and making the Breath of Oðin flow from the core of the Self through the physical, merging with the Megin and flowing into the Hamingja's form as new divinely empowered Megin. If it is the only thing you ever do, master this well. It is THAT important. The final step will be covered in the geometric Fylgja teachings but for it to function, this divinely empowered individualised Megin is needed first.

Empowered Runic Vocalisation

Having worked with your Hamingja and awoken the Breath of Oðin, it is now possible to add a second dimension to your rune vocalisations. Previously, when chanting the runes, meditating with them or applying them in charged bind-runes, only one aspect of the runic flow was used. This involved pulling in the characteristics of the runic current of each rune. It can be thought of as imbuing what you are doing with the properties of each rune (or what they represent, the scope of influences they have, their functions). If ᚠ Fé (Fehu) is used, you would focus on its fiery aspects, the power (amount) of luck and money and circulating wealth. However, what is missing in these types of applications is the power (or substance) aspect of the runic flow. This is the dynamism of runic power.

As seen during the practices undertaken so far, the Megin is the power side of this equation. It has not been applied so far. Now it is time to add this missing element into the rune work, adding an extra 'kick' so to speak. Thinking of it in elemental terms, the typical rune use links to the air element, the vocalisation and transmission of properties (or characteristics) of each rune. Adding the Hamingja and Megin in order to 'dynamise' the runic flow allows you to include the power (fire) elemental influence to the rune, which adds a second dimension to the practice and immediately activating the rune chants since now both activating principles (fire and air) are set in motion.

Megin-empowered Rune Chanting

In this practice, you will be making actual use of the personified Hamingja in order to empower the chanted runes. Its main goal is to familiarise yourself with both the manipulation of Megin and work with the Hamingja.

Start by relaxing and shifting awareness into the Hamingja. As you do so, step out in its form and stand behind your physical body (Lik). Feel the Megin flowing within the Hamingja, whilst also keeping hold of your awareness of the physical. Select a rune to work with. Focus on it whilst maintaining your awareness in both the physical

Megin used to empower runic vocalisation

and Hamingja. Meditate on what the rune represents and why you are using it. At this point, the characteristics flowing through that rune's current are being connected with and called upon.

Having established a firm grip on the qualitative side of the rune, use your physical body (Lik) to chant out its name, allowing your awareness to be flooded with how it sounds, how it makes your vocal cords vibrate and how it feels. This will ground the characteristics of the rune during meditation. Shift your focus into the personified Hamingja, and feel the Megin flowing within it anew. Establishing this sensory perception is key. Once you have achieved this, vocalise the rune's name from within the personified Hamingja, feeling the vibration of that name and willing it to be charged with Megin flowing from within the Hamingja. You will notice that this feels powerful; it is almost comparable to having a solid sound wave bursting forth from the mouth of the personified Hamingja. Here the characteristics of the runic flow are irrelevant; it is the power that matters instead.

Quick Steps

1   Relax and allow the world to fade from awareness.

2   Step out of the physical body (Lik) in your Hamingja preserving awareness and focus within it.

3   Feel the Megin flowing within the Hamingja and re-focus on the physical, also preserving your sense of the physical.

4   Select a rune to work with. At first, it is best to pick one you are comfortable with and feel close to. Meditate on the rune, its meaning for

you and what you think its energy is all about. Here you focus on the characteristics of the runic energy whilst maintaining awareness of both the Hamingja and the physical.

5   Now chant the rune; feel the vibration of its name, what it sounds like, how it feels, keeping in mind the characteristics of the rune you meditated on a few instants ago. You are literally vocalising it.

6   Next, focus on the personified Hamingja, feel the Megin within it, vocalise the rune from the Hamingja and feel the sound vibrations emanating from the Hamingja (NOT the physical body (Lik)). It feels like a solid sound wave bursting with Megin matching the type of rune used (a little like a flavouring of the Megin with runic energy).

7   Following on from this, the next step is to synchronise the two vocalisations, work up to the point where you eventually are vocalising the rune both physically (expressing its properties or characteristics) and, via the Hamingja (expressing its power).

The trick with this practice is to keep at it until you are able to simultaneously do the physical and the Hamingja parts. In other words, this involves vocalising the rune from the personified Hamingja, feeling that solid sound wave type of bursting Megin AND simultaneously chanting it from the physical body (Lik), feeling the characteristics (or properties, meanings, influences . . .) of the same rune. Getting skilled in this is essential; it will literally empower your runic chants and increase their effectiveness incredibly. You should aim to master this until both the characteristics of the rune being vocalised and the power (Megin fuelled) synchronise properly. This is the first step to proper genuine runic vocalisation, in other words: actual Galdr.

DUAL-FORM RUNIC VOCALISATION

The previous practice will have assisted in developing your familiarity in working from within the Hamingja as well as merging the characteristics and the powers of runic vocalisation. The following one will increase these abilities and allow you to achieve the same effect whilst being in your body; in other words, the vocal cords of your physical body (Lik) will channel not only the characteristics of the rune vocalisation but will also be used to deal with its power(s).

Start by relaxing and allow the world to fade away from your immediate conscious awareness. Shift into the personified Hamingja, but do not stay behind the physical body (Lik); instead, merge with it whilst maintaining the separation of both forms (in other words, as during the earlier practices when awakening the Breath of Oðin, do not allow the physical and the Hamingja to merge). Keep them both separate but within the same form and space.

Feel the Hamingja's Megin and the physical body (Lik); feel their connection, how the one flows through the other. This is then followed by taking in one single full Breath of Oðin (inflow and outflow), ensuring the personalised empowered Megin flows from the core of the Self, via the DNA and infusing the Megin. Maintain this personalised Megin and will it to flow through your blood, then through all the parts of the physical body until it fills each and every molecule of your very body. Concentrate on your throat; feel the vocal cords and allow the Megin to concentrate there. Do not do this for too long; the stronger the focus and the more energy you allow to accumulate there, the more tension it will create in the throat. Start with as little as possible then work up the level of tension you allow. No point in harming your body; you need it! Once you are comfortable with feeling the Megin concentrated in your throat (more specifically, your vocal cords), utter the rune to be vocalised.

This part is trickier than in the previous practice. Here you need to ensure you are meditating on the characteristics / properties of the runes, keeping full awareness of the personified Hamingja, focusing on the physical body (Lik), concentrating on the Megin and directing the outburst of runic-infused Megin as you vocalise the selected rune.

Quick Steps

1 Start by relaxing and shifting your awareness into the Hamingja as you step out of your physical body (Lik). Split your awareness into both forms. Step into the physical so that you are occupying the same space in both bodies as you should be used to from previous practices.

2 Feel how the two forms are connected, Megin flowing from the one through the other, the blood from the physical pushing the flow of Megin and vice versa.

3 Do a full Breath of Oðin (one in-breath and one out-breath), ensuring that the personalised Megin is flowing from the Spark of Self via the DNA back through the blood and imbuing each and every molecule / cell of your body and the Hamingja.

4 Concentrate on your physical throat, and at the same time keep aware of the Hamingja's throat. As you focus your dual awareness into both throats, the empowered Megin will concentrate in those regions in both forms. You should feel a strong pulse there. Do not overdo it.

5 Keeping the vocal cords in focus, chant the rune name. Feel the burst of Megin-charged sound emanate from the Hamingja as you do so, and feel the characteristics of the rune burst forth in the same instant from the physical.

6 Practice as much as possible; the multiple foci of awareness, the meditation on the qualities and the feeling of the powers flowing, all need to be maintained simultaneously.

Practice makes perfect. Mastering this is critical for proper Galdr. Do not despair; mastery will arrive for those who practice and persist.

May the glory of the mysteries of the North unveiled be! With many thanks to Oðin, Húnir and Lóðurr ...

This, ladies and gents in Midgard, completes the teachings on developing the Hamingja for the time being. More will be forthcoming in future titles but they will all rely on the work and foundations established herein. Enjoy and I do wish you the best of luck! And guidance from the Ásgarðians who smile upon their children ...

Frank A. Rúnaldrar

APPENDIXES

APPENDIX A

TABLE OF RUNIC NAMES IN ICELANDIC & GERMANIC

Rune	Numeric Value	Icelandic Name	Germanic Name
ᚠ	1	Fé	Fehu
ᚢ	2	Úr	Uruz
ᚦ	3	Þurs	Thurisaz
ᚨ	4	Óss (Ás)	Ansuz
ᚱ	5	Reið	Raidho
ᚲ	6	Kaun	Kenaz
ᚷ	7	Gjöf	Gebo
ᚹ	8	Vin	Wunjo
ᚺ	9	Hagall	Hagalaz
ᚾ	10	Nauð	Nauthiz
ᛁ	11	Íss	Isa
ᛃ	12	Ár	Jera
ᛈ	13	Perð	Pertho
ᛇ	14	Jór	Eihwaz
ᛉ	15	Ýr	Elhaz
ᛋ	16	Sól	Sowilo
ᛏ	17	Týr	Tiwaz
ᛒ	18	Bjarkan	Berkano
ᛖ	19	Eykur	Ehwaz
ᛗ	20	Maður	Mannaz
ᛚ	21	Lögur	Laguz
ᛜ	22	Ing	Ingwaz
ᛞ	23	Dagur	Dagaz
ᛟ	24	Óðal	Othala

APPENDIX B

References & footnotes

1. Strange Footprints on the Land (Author: Irwin, Constance publisher: Harper & Row, 1980) ISBN 0-06-022772-9)

2. Snorri Sturluson. The Prose Edda: Tales from Norse Mythology, translated by Jean I. Young (University of California Press, 1964)

3. Denali Institute of Northern Traditions (2003). Handbook of Rune Mentalist Skills, Alaska: Northbooks, p.38

4. Scudder, Bernard (1997). 'Egil's Saga'. In Hreinsson, Viðar. The Complete Sagas of Icelanders Including 49 Tales. Volume 1. Reykjavík: Leifur Eiríksson. ISBN_9979929308.

5. G.Dumézil (1970), p. 142

6. Denali Institute of Northern Traditions (2003). Handbook of Rune Mentalist Skills, Alaska: Northbooks, p.39

7. Scudder, Bernard (1997). 'Egil's Saga'. In Hreinsson, Viðar. The Complete Sagas of Icelanders Including 49 Tales. Volume 1. Reykjavík: Leifur Eiríksson. ISBN_9979929308.

8. Denali Institute of Northern Traditions (2003). Handbook of Rune Mentalist Skills, Alaska: Northbooks, p.38

9. Simon J. Greenhill; Ross Clark; Bruce Biggs (2010). 'Protoform: MANA.1 [OC] Power, effectiveness, pres-

tige'. Polynesian Lexicon Project Online.

10. Bruce Biggs (1965). Polynesian Lexicon Project Online.

11. Blust, Robert (2007). 'Proto-Oceanic *mana Revisited'. Oceanic Linguistics 36 (2): 404-422.

12. Codrington, R. H. (1891). The Melanesians: Studies in Their Anthropology and Folklore. Oxford: Clarendon Press. p._118

13. Marett, R.R. (1914) [1909]. The Threshold of Religion (Second, Revised and Enlarged, ed.). London: Methuen and Co. Ltd.

14. Ante p. 2.

15. Ante p. 14-15.

16. Hewitt, J. N. B. (1902). 'Orenda and a Definition of Religion'. American Anthropologist 4 (1): 33-46.

17. Ante p. 41.

18. Ante p. 42.

19. Rose, Herbert Jennings (1951). 'Nvmen and Mana'. Harvard Theological Review 44 (3): 109-120.

20. Ante p. 37.

21. Ante p. 38.

22. Marett, R.R. (1914) [1909]. The Threshold of Religion (Second, Revised and Enlarged ed.). London: Methuen and Co. Ltd. p. 12-13.

SUGGESTED FURTHER READING

Kevin Crossley-Holland (2011) 'The Penguin Book of Norse Myths: Gods of the Vikings'. London: Penguin Books ISBN 978-0-241-95321-1

Lee M. Hollander (2012) The Poetic Edda, Texas: University of Texas Press ISBN: 978-0-292-76499-6

Snorri Sturlson. Translated by: Arthur Gilchrist Brodeur (2014) 'The Prose Edda' CreateSpace ISBN 978-1500104948

Snorri Sturluson (2008) 'Edda (Everyman)', W&N; New Ed edition ISBN 978-0460876162

W H Auden (2010) 'Havamal Words of the High One' USA: Kessinger Publishing ISBN 978-1169174139

OTHER TITLES
BY FRANK A. RÚNALDRAR

The Breath of Oðin Awakens
Questions & Answers Ed.

(ISBN: 978-0-9955343-1-5)

The essential guide and companion to 'The Breath of Oðin Awakens' looks at readers' questions, issues, difficulties and experiences. It provides direct guidance on many of the most common and complex issues raised.

You will be guided through some of the most frequently encountered hurdles, sticking points and draw benefit from essential pointers on how to overcome these challenges. In addition, you will read some of the most interesting reports, feedback and in some cases life changing experiences of other readers shared with the public for the first time.

For those that are more curious than others, a carefully selected handful of practices that were omitted from 'The Breath of Oðin Awakens' are included within, in response to readers' queries.

Some of the topics discussed include, healing with Megin, enhancing physical recovery, increasing personal wealth, examples of runic pathing, expanding on mental and spiritual abilities and using the increase of luck for specific life events and many more...

THE SPIRIT OF HÚNIR AWAKENS (PART 1)
Norse Keys to Spirit, Mind & Perception
(ISBN: 978-0-9955343-2-2)

Spirit, Mind and Perception – these three fundamental components of consciousness are impossibly hard to define and little understood. Yet, they are so critically essential to our very beings.

Have you ever thought it strange that so much has been written about the spirit, the mind and our perceptions, yet still the practical knowledge and insights that would enable mastery remain inaccessible? Have you ever wondered what it would be like to be of pure perception or to consciously act from within your spirit? To strip your perception of illusions or perceive beyond the purely physical?

Discover the secrets of the Spirit (Óðr), Mind (Hugr) and Memory (Minni). Draw from simple and effective practices to develop your perceptions, enhance your senses, take control of your mind, expand consciousness beyond the purely physical and act from within your spirit. Learn to feed, grow and expand your Spirit's innate potential.

Immerse yourself in the knowledge found within the Norse tradition to master these key parts of your Self. Start discovering who and what you actually are, what you are capable of! Awaken to the full power of Your Spirit!

THE SPIRIT OF HÚNIR AWAKENS (PART 2)
The Norse 'Holy Grail'
(ISBN: 978-0-9955343-2-2)

Unlock your Consciousness and unfold the full potential of your awareness! Start understanding how thought functions and how to shape your Self within the reality around you. Master the innate nature of your Spirit.

Have you ever wondered why you think in a specific way? Why you end up stuck in endless pointless loops of negative thought? Or perhaps why everything seems so hopeless while others around you are not bound by such thinking? Break free by understanding how to defeat these patterns and vanquish the Mind Thief, unlocking the actual power of thought and manipulating it to your advantage in all you do!

Your memories hold phenomenal resources of which you can take advantage. Learn how to make practical use of them for both empowerment and healing. Rid yourself of memories which hinder you in life and use them instead to your advantage through mastery of the Minni.

Discover how the runes will help you to reclaim your energies and enhance your awareness through runic trance dancing. Learn the proper methods for visualisation and master the actual power of intent and pure thought, the keys to shaping reality through your Will, and realise the hidden potential of the Norse 'Holy Grail'.

FORTHCOMING
TITLES

THE BLOOD OF LÓÐURR AWAKENS
Power of the Midgard Man

The blood, DNA, flesh and physicality of our bodies are taken for granted by countless humans and envied by many others. We, the children of Yggdrasil (world tree) to whom Midgard (physical reality) was given at the time of our creation, hold deep and powerful secrets within ourselves and within our physical beings.

The Body (Lik), the Energy Body (Hamr) and the Shadow (Sal) form the great foundation of our own inner universe: our own creation. Understanding and master-ing these physical parts of our Self provides us with such wonderful gifts that there are those in Creation who positively fear the prospect of our self-realisation.

The deep-seated secrets of centrality and balance are but a few of the wonders which await the reader. Mysteries of materialisation, realisation through inheritance and mysteries of our very blood will be revealed to all.

Learn all about their practical applications, their secrets and how to expand your Self through their proper use. Learn how to ground and materialise runic powers through them, how to manifest events in life by means of these three physical parts of your Self and learn why mankind is the envy of Creation.

High Galdr: Rune Science
The Sacred Science of the Gods

Runes, runes and more runes! The sacred science of the Gods, the runes were made available to their children, our Ancestors. Much information is available about the runes, yet so very little is known as to how they are actually used. They are chanted, they are written, and they are drawn. Yet all these methods fail to produce rapid or tangible manifestations.

Using the runes is a science and, like any science, the rules under which its principles operate need to be known. Unleashing a runic vocalisation using proper Galdr has been kept secret for ages, known to only an extremely select few who were capable of mastering their very Self. These methods for Galdr were passed down through generations as part of our vocal tradition, with only sparse written instruction preserved.

At long last, actual methods and underlying principles of manifesting the power of the runes are being made available unabridged with no hidden facets, no secret methods left unturned. Learn at long last how to wield the runes, how to unleash and manifest them, how to recode reality and reform events in life using the heritage left to us by our Ancestors and living with-in our DNA. Each and every rune holds a secret, a key, a power, a source of knowledge and a potential.

Learn to unleash it ALL with actual High Galdr.

Printed in February 2024
by Rotomail Italia S.p.A., Vignate (MI) - Italy